To A New D

Letters of S

Editor's note

The following letters are published largely unedited. We have, however, made some soft edits to clarify meaning where required, for the benefit of the reader. We have not sought to alter the voices represented in this anthology, and we have taken measures to preserve the powerful, thoughtful and insightful voices of the young people whose letters are featured within these pages.

To A New Dawn

Letters of Solidarity

Edited by Eve Makis

THE EMMA PRESS

Copyright

Project administered by Nottingham UNESCO City of Literature, with funding and support from Arts Council England, Nottingham Castle Trust, Nottingham Trent University and the Thomas Farr Charity.

Print ISBN 978-1-912915-76-7
eBook ISBN 978-1-912915-77-4

A CIP catalogue record of this book is available from the British Library.

Printed and bound in the UK by Imprint Digital, Exeter.

Typeset by Emma Dai'an Wright

Published by The Emma Press
theemmapress.com

Contents

Acknowledgements

We would like to thank all the writers who contributed letters and extracts of letters to the Letters of Solidarity project and to this anthology: your words are moving, insightful and hopeful, and we're delighted to showcase your work. We are grateful to Richard Bromhall for organising the Letters of Solidarity project and to Ruby Tyler for making the website look incredible.

To Eve Makis for her excellent work editing the anthology, and to our volunteer editing assistants: Anna Friel, Callum Roome, Daria Paterek, Emma Stirland, Kishan Ganatra, Marie-Laure Corben, Katie Moore, Molly Whitford, Rijuta Lutchegadoo and Zoe Nevin – thank you for your thoughtful and empathetic editing support on the project. To Emma Dai'an Wright and the team at the Emma Press for putting together such a beautiful publication that fully celebrates the voices of the writers within it. And to Dr Sarah McConnell and Chris Brown at Nottingham Trent University for supporting Kira Betts to design our fabulous cover art for the anthology.

We are deeply grateful to receive funding and ongoing support for this project from Arts Council England, Nottingham Castle Trust, Nottingham Trent University and the Thomas Farr Charity. Thank you for allowing us to elevate the voices of young people in our city.

We are also unbelievably grateful to you, the reader. 2020 has been an incredibly challenging year but, as this project has shown, there is always hope.

Nottingham UNESCO City of Literature, December 2020

www.nottinghamcityofliterature.com

Introduction

There's something wonderfully unique about young voices. An honesty and fearlessness, a strong belief in a better future, anger expressed without apology, a desire to spearhead change. Hope shone through the letters in our anthology, even when very dark emotions were expressed. We have letters to and from Covid-19. Letters of appreciation to mums, friends and key workers. One writer escaped lockdown through literature, another through her obsession with online maths. An NHS father wrote to his unborn son.

Many young people expressed concerns about racism, the environment and the prospect of joblessness. We received letters about depression, loneliness and a funeral in lockdown, the healing power of FaceTime with friends. In these pages you will find empathy, humour and wise words in abundance.

To A New Dawn was written and edited almost exclusively by young people. Our team of editors discussed what solidarity meant to them, and here's what they had to say:

Solidarity is a catch-up over a cup of tea and a gentle nod of understanding. A rejection of the things that divide us and a celebration of what makes us individual.

It's connectedness: through experience, through values, through standing with others in their struggles. It's resilience in the face of adversity. A feeling that you are not alone: a smile, a reply, an acknowledgement. The willingness to provide aid as well as make people feel safe. It is all-encompassing, from small acts of kindness in student communities, to coming together to fight injustice. Solidarity lies in the little gestures – the small things we do every day to show people we love and support them. It's sending a text to check in with a far-away friend, and calling grandparents to brighten their day.

Our anthology is an act of solidarity, capturing a singular moment in history and reflecting the irrepressible spirit of youth.

Eve Makis, December 2020

About our editor: Eve Makis is the author of four novels, a screenplay and a life writing guide. She teaches fiction on the MA in Creative Writing at Nottingham Trent University, where she is writer-in-residence for the Postcolonial Studies Centre.

EMANI, 19

To a New Dawn,

When lockdown hit, we were all plunged into darkness. Not as a creeping shadow – we did not get the luxury of time – but rather a plunge into an icy lake with rocks around our feet. Rocks that were built from our fear of the unknown, the loss of loved ones and ourselves.

Everyone's icy lake looked different, but mine took shape as a room with four simple walls. My home was 5,215 miles away, so the four walls of my accommodation became my new family. At first, they kept me safe, my protection against the darkness that blanketed our city, cradling me in their warmth and standing there with unfaltering stability.

They saw me laugh, they saw me cry, but then I stopped doing either; although the walls kept out the darkness, they did not stop it from budding inside the empty landscape of my heart and mind. It sprouted as spring moved into summer and within days it was an impenetrable, twisted wall of ivy, wrapped around me like the duvet I called my new home.

The thought of no foreseeable future plagued my mind, a plague that had become, perhaps, even more contagious to the minds of students than the virus that had placed us in isolation. Then, as I tossed and turned with restlessness into the early hours, the four walls felt as though they were betraying me, and in a desperate escape I went outside. That's when I saw that the darkness that had filled the empty streets had been broken by you.

You rose, a beacon of hope and solidarity. Claps for the NHS and music in the park became our Aubade, the sounds of which filled my ears and consequently filtered out the dark clouds of my mind. We were all reciting the same words, singing the same tunes, and because of that the streets of Nottingham were never truly empty when they were greeted by you.

Together we know that, when the night comes back to claim us, we will create a new dawn to pull us out once more.

Love from us.

Emani

"I love the sensitive exploration of the mental toll of lockdown in this letter, as well as its emerging hopeful message. The depiction of the people of Nottingham coming together in the final paragraph is a beautiful image of local solidarity."

Molly Whitford, Volunteer Editor

An aubade is a poem or a piece of music appropriate to the dawn or early morning.

RAE, 16

The silence has changed me and maybe it has changed us all. Change is scary, untrusted, but it is not as terrible as it appears; it gives us opportunity, growth, creativity, freedom.

DANIEL, 25

To my Unborn Son,

I wake up in the mornings, frosty and cold. Where did the night go? I rub my eyes; it doesn't help. Never does. I'm still tired, vision blurry. I put on my glasses. Better. I fumble for the lamplight. A warm, orange glow, just enough to function but careful not to disturb your mum. She's snoring. You're kicking; I can feel your thumps as I whisper good morning to my little man. I rip off my PJs and pull up my work slacks. The cold was never my friend. I remind myself: there are more lives to save.

I stuff lunch into my rucksack bag. I make a mental note to thank Mum for making it when I get home. Automatically, I tip cornflakes into an old, chipped bowl and splash in milk. I munch and prepare. Joints stiff, brain still foggy… What now? Shirt! I button up my shirt in reverence. This is my uniform. I don my NHS lanyard and slide on my grandpa's old Clarks. Comfiest shoes you did ever know. I hope he'd be proud. Management plans for my patients edge slowly to the fore. I'm fond of them; I hate to see them admitted but love to see them leave. I pray I can help reunite more with their families today. Grasping the doorknob, I boldly step across the threshold demarcating my flat and the outside world. At home I'm Daniel, a husband and expectant father. I love to goof off, and dad jokes come naturally. But as I look up, seeing only the stars pinpricking the pitch blackness, out here I'm a medical student. The gravitas of which sometimes feels too heavy.

The keys fumble in my numb fingers. I promise myself one day I'll buy a car with remote locking. Folded into the car, the engine brums to life. Cooed by the engine's ancient rhythm, steady judder, and the smell of old furniture, the old dog comes to life.

I have little over a year to go before I'm a junior doctor, but already I feel the trust people put in me. I ask them questions and they give me intimate answers, unflinchingly. Affairs, misdeeds, regrets: I delicately hold them all. Mould them into diagnoses I proffer to my consultants. I hold his hands as the retired doctor prepares for chemo. He looks up at me for reassurance; I squeeze tighter. I listen as a woman tells me she has months to live; her husband's face tenses, pained. It hangs low. I dedicate my break time to looking into palliative care; my textbook is dotted with tear marks.

So many have died recently, and I have felt so useless. Covid-19 has scorched communities, scarring countries like the bushfires did in Australia. Political calamity is divisive, spurring national in-fighting; children are starving during a pandemic, while ethnic minorities are fighting to simply… matter. I'd hoped to welcome you into better circumstances. I want justice, I want healing, I want a world as hungry for equality as for dominance.

I slow into my parking spot. In the midst of despair, I remember: I can't lift the world, but I can lift where I stand. I look forward to lifting you up to reach your dreams. Suddenly, my world is alright. I can't be everything to everyone, but I can be something to someone. I double-check I've got everything and rapidly open the glove box to find my stethoscope smiling at me. I wondered where it had gone.

I'm greeted by Annabelle at the door, offering a crisp blue mask and hand sanitiser. I smile. She can't see it, but I think she smiles back. I've crossed another threshold. My home away from home. Even in lockdown, our voices cannot be shut down. Our actions ripple, albeit subtly. As humanity ever-incessantly grinds at the limits of possibility, so must I donate my might, hoping one day, not far from now, I will save lives and you can be proud of me.

Love always,

Your NHS Dad

"The profoundly moving nature of this NHS Dad's letter caught me off guard: from the narrator's role as an expectant father to a dutiful and attentive medical student, it is their care that has helped so many during this pandemic. Examples of such devotion are the greatest display of solidarity."

Anna Friel, Volunteer Editor

BEATRICE MUNRO, 17

When I thought what a 'letter of solidarity' might entail, I was struck by the enormity of such a task. I cannot possibly hope to encompass a universal experience. So I will stick to what I know, and hope that my individual experience might be enlightening.

Lockdown was inequal parts anxiety to calm. It was like strong squash: more enjoyable than it had any right to be, but nevertheless pungently overpowering. I am now in my last year of school, and so watched this year's exam results fiasco with trepidation. Autumn brought the tumult of students going to university – where I hope to be next year – and that only increased my fear and anxiety. Returning to school has been a blessing, however. I have been reminded of a useful mantra: worry about what you can control; do not fret about what you cannot. Thus I am in the process of creating a zen-like state to attempt to salvage my mental health as the days draw in.

But I don't entirely fear the longer nights. Waking up to a dark window in the morning has its magic; walking to school under a rising sun wondrous. I also relish the brisk and still air of winter, rosy cheeks and ruffled hat-hair being the marks of a good walk. I also enjoy seeing the world at night, despite how afraid I am of it sometimes. Everything is set in a mellow light, a sepia tone rendering it magical. Night-time walks have become a fixture to banish my grown-up night terrors.

In solidarity, I offer my story, my experience and my hope for the future. Nottingham will always be a love, its people unique. So I raise my cup of squash in solidarity; tentative, but not fearful, of what is to come.

"Solidarity… in one letter? It's exactly what Beatrice highlights here: an enormous task. But what she writes, her individual experience, is enlightening and serves as part of the whole anthology connecting people's lives to express our solidarity. Beatrice makes me feel invited to also enjoy life's simple pleasures, and her running metaphor of a strong squash adds a comic yet heartfelt tone as she closes her letter, hopeful of the future."

Katie Moore, Volunteer Editor

DEANNA EL KHOURY, 18

Nottingham
25th July 2020

Big Umi (Zainab Bibi)
Al-Jannah

Dear Big Umi,

I am with you now at Chadderton Cemetery. My uncle, Ajmal, and my auntie, Bashshas, are here. And my grandmother (your daughter), whom I have always called Umi, stands with us too. I stand alongside my parents and my brother, yet I feel as though I am standing the furthest away from your grave.

Your grave. It is a forest of flowers that my relatives have planted for you. And at the top is a little plaque stuck into the mound of soil. You will have this plaque until the gravestone has been made for you. It reads:

'In Loving Memory ZAINAB BIBI Born 07/06/1931 Passed Away 24/04/2020.'

Of course, we don't exactly know when you were born – I hope we didn't get it too wrong.

Aged 18 and I still call you by the name invented for you before I was even born. As you know, Umi means 'mum' in Urdu. I began calling your daughter Umi at family gatherings when I heard other relatives refer to her in that way, even though she is my grandmother. I don't know who called you 'Big Umi' first, but it soon caught on.

Now, regardless of where they are in the family tree, everyone calls you Big Umi.

We are in the Muslim section of the cemetery. Close by, two men are praying in Arabic over the grave of a woman who also died in April. As I read *Surah Yasīn* over my mum's shoulder, furrowing my eyebrows at unfamiliar Arabic letters and stumbling over the archaic English translation, I feel as though I was not close to you at all.

I feel incredibly bad that I didn't get to know you when you were alive. I had this grand plan: when I finished my A-level exams in late June – exams that never took place – I was going to spend time this summer learning more Urdu-Punjabi Mix (what Umi calls the language you would speak to one another). I wanted to do this so that I could really talk to you. Or at least so that I could do more than smile at you, only able to say and understand *asalaam-alaykum*, *gee* Big Umi, *nae* Big Umi and *khudha hafiz* (that's a way of saying goodbye, readers).

I should have tried to make more of an effort when I was younger. Not just to learn more words, but to ask you more questions too. Even if we would not have understood each other well, Umi could have helped. She could have told you what I wanted to ask, and then she could have explained to me what you had said.

But instead, each time we exchanged smiles and kisses on cheeks before I left your house – *khudha hafiz*, Big Umi – I would know nothing more about you than I did before.

A
fall,
a thunder-clap headache,
a day in hospital with no visitors permitted and a last breath in your house
later and it was too late.

You died on the first day of Ramadan. Around the time of evening when Muslims break their fast.

Good fortune – during Ramadan, all doors to hell are shut.

We are standing together by your graveside. In my head, I am saying sorry to you – sorry, sorry, sorry, you meant more to me than a part of my routine greetings when entering and leaving your house. I am not sure whether you can hear me or not, but I hope you do know this.

Although many of us could not attend your funeral, as a maximum of ten people were allowed, Umi made sure that your funeral happened the day after your death. So you can rest knowing that your body was never in a mortuary.

Yesterday, I asked Umi how she would describe you.

"I think she was very gentle… she didn't harm anybody if she could help it. Sort of very forgiving. Sort of a happy type of person," Umi said, as she stood by the kitchen stove cooking *roti* that she would later use to make *chorri*. And I wondered what you thought about this country. How did you feel when you first came to live here? And when we visited – chatting and interrupting each other, asking for the fruit bowl, the nuts, offering tea, all in a chorus of English – what was that like for you?

I know you would not have been able to read my letter. But by writing this, I hope you know that I care for you more than I showed when you were alive.

I stand with Bashshas as she finishes reading *Surah Yasīn* from the booklet she's holding. Everyone else has started to make their way back to the cars. I turn around to find a few more rows of graves, younger than yours. In the newest row, I can see a family gathered round one of the piles of earth. One of the children is tending to the grave with a watering can, while the woman holds her hands in prayer and the man sits on a chair to one side. It is 25th July, just three months and one day after you died, and so many new graves already?

Bashshas and I check that we're both alright before moving away from your grave. As we walk down the aisle between two congregations of black stone, earth and flowers, we notice how many rows of graves we pass belong to people who have died during lockdown. I fall silent as I think of all these lives lost, many of which must be to Covid-19. As we continue to walk down the path, all together now, I realise how lucky we have all been. Lucky that you died at home – your wish. Lucky to have had a great grandmother in my lifetime, all of us fortunate to have spent so much time with you. I am so very glad to have known you, and I hope that I can learn more about you through the stories of my other relatives.

I will always miss your smile.

Khudha hafiz, Big Umi.

Deanna

"Beautifully written and deeply personal, Deanna's tribute to her great grandmother really moved me while also ending on a poignant note of hope and positivity in celebrating her life. Well done – Big Umi would be proud of you!"

Marie-Laure Corben, Volunteer Editor

HOLLIE, 19

A Letter to myself, at the start of the pandemic.

Dear Me,

You're probably wondering why I'm writing this to you. It's me, well… it's you, 7 months later and with much cooler hair. You'll be surprised that Covid-19 is still dictating our lives. I'm sure you think your life right now is confusing, with the serious relationship ending, the dropping out of sixth form and so on. This is bad, granted, but please be prepared for it all to get much worse.

You'll be shocked to hear that, upon one spontaneous drunk FaceTime call at 1am, you pack up and move out of your parent's house, subsequently moving into a flatshare with a friend, a friend who will soon reveal their true colours. She's not who you believed her to be and she's not a good friend for you. Stop seeing the good in people who you realistically know aren't good! You idiot.

Right now you're eighteen years old, and unequivocally the idea of freedom to this extent is exciting. You're going to meet an array of interesting people, to say the least. Lots of tears and laughs are going to be present in this period. While we are on the topic of this period, stop picking up his calls, I know you know who I am talking about, yes him, it's not worth it. You'll find out why in a few months. Pre-cue the Kelly Clarkson now, trust me.

Tell your mum you love her; you're only going to see her once a week for a picnic in your front garden. Remember that this woman does more for you than you will ever appreciate. Please at least attempt to show you care now; me and you both know she deserves the world, and you're going to put her through a lot these coming months.

A lot of events are going to take place that will leave you a shell of a human; a lot of ups and downs that will leave you all over the place. For example, you're going to move out of the flat and into a house share on your own, you're going to nearly die in hospital due to your own actions, with your mum by your side fearing for your life (see what I said about putting that woman through a lot!), and something very bad is going to happen. It's going to destroy you. It's so bad that I'm not going to tell you what it is. All I'll say is please remember that, as Rupi Kaur said, it "will tear you apart, but it will not end you", because it will tear you in half but will to teach you to love, accept and value yourself, the person who you are and meant to be.

I love you.

From You, October 2020

MATTHEW BENTON-SMITH, 16

To Key Workers,

This letter is from me to you, but not directly. This letter comes from a whole nation that you have fought for through unprecedented times, and, where possible, kept the land of hope and glory smiling.

To the NHS staff rushed off their feet with hospital admissions, fighting daily for people's lives throughout some of the toughest and most testing times in the history of the country; through the unbearable beeping of lifesaving machines and the deafening cries of patients. Being the first and sadly sometimes the last friendly face that far too many people saw during their battle with Covid-19. You gave the population a reason to come together, albeit at a distance. Every Thursday night at 7pm the streets would be bursting with pride, as we all put a hand together for you. Although we can sadly never fully repay you for your work like we wish we could, we all came together to show you how thankful we are, that we cared, and that you were in our thoughts at this loathsome time.

To the shop workers braving the possibility of exposure to the virus that stopped the world but couldn't stop you from keeping a fragmented United Kingdom stocked up. Speaking to us with a smile as we queued outside the store, that short period of social interaction that we were otherwise deprived of. You may not realise it, but you made many people's day, young and old, as we finally got the chance to step out from the strained relationships in our household bubbles to see a new face. It was a time when you were fighting many battles: against coronavirus, against panic buyers, and at many times against yourselves as you found courage not to give up. As the Great British saying goes, "Keep Calm and Carry On."

To the bus drivers who made sure that the wheels kept turning and people kept moving. You helped people be on time and keep their jobs at a time when many others unfortunately couldn't. You kept going through a period that was different to any other: no traffic on the roads would usually be a blessing, something that usually only happened in your wildest dreams but at this time was a daily reminder of the isolation we were facing. I would have loved nothing more than to have seen a bustling city and be sat in the rush hour traffic I once cursed every day. But you kept going, and for that we thank you.

To the teachers who worked tirelessly to keep our young people educated, whether you were locked up at home or fearlessly heading into school grounds to teach the vulnerable. At a time when many children would have quite happily sat by as all their commitments and studies casually drifted out of their minds, you helped to enlighten the key workers and world leaders of tomorrow.

To anyone and everyone who kept the world moving at a time when it could easily have come to a swift halt. From myself, and the whole of our fabulous nation… it's more than just a simple thank you; it's a national salute.

From,

Matthew Benton-Smith

"This wonderfully-written letter is a heartfelt and important nod to all the people that keep the world spinning on a daily basis. I appreciate the emphasis it puts on the importance of being grateful for even the simplest of gestures, such as a smile in the supermarket queue."

Zoe Nevin, Volunteer Editor

CHARLIE DAWN-SADLER, 23

For Women, unconditionally,

During lockdown, like thousands of us around the country, I found myself a new hobby. A lifelong lover of literature, I decided to share my thoughts, recommendations and book reviews in video format to YouTube. This niche little corner of the site is affectionately referred to as 'BookTube', a great space for people to excitedly share their bookish opinions with other bibliophiles.

After editing and double checking, processing and loading, I was eager to see the kind of reaction I would get. Three minutes later, I found out. A comment, woohoo! What does it say? What did they think? In large capital letters, the comment reads: "LOSE WEIGHT FATTY!!"

Now, at 23 years old and with a lifetime of fat-shaming under my belt, I chuckled and guffawed at the surprise of it. After texting my friends and hilariously sharing it to my Instagram story, it got me thinking: what effect would this have had on me five years ago? Would I have burst into laughter or tears?

For some, a comment like that could send them plummeting into the depths of self-conscious loathing. Comments like these are demeaning, cruel and intentionally harmful; they are all these things and more, but one thought twisted through my mind again and again: why?

I wondered less about why the anonymous commenter would say that to me (people have their own bizarre excuses for doing all sorts of things, and you can't apply reason to unreasonable people) but more about why those specific words could be used to hurt my feelings. Why have words like *fat, pig, cow, fatty, big, chubby, heffa* and all the other schoolyard taunts we've heard before caused such riots in our minds? Because we have learned that Fat is less than, Fat is ugly, and there is no room for beauty in Fat. For one moment I want you to imagine that this is true, that Fat really does equal unattractive, undesirable, unwanted. For a second moment I want you to think about this: are attractive, desirable and wanted the best things you could be? For a third moment I want you to answer: who says attractiveness, desirability and wanting are a must, a necessity, a requirement of being a woman?

Is Fat ugly? Is Fat beautiful? Or are neither of those things conditional to the other?

We can, and do, sustain ourselves on much more than just beauty. So, if there is no obligation to be beautiful, be whatever makes your skin glow from the inside out. Once you take away their power to dictate what you should and must be, you gain the power to unapologetically be yourself. If being a woman has no superficial beauty conditions attached, then their name calling, their taunts, are nothing more than words falling on deaf ears, echoing back to themselves.

Yours sincerely,

Charlie-Dawn Sadler

ZOE CHINDA, 17

Dear Racism,

I'm glad you're scared. I'm glad that you've had a bad year. We all have. People are dead because of you, but the name GEORGE FLOYD will forever be on our minds since you took him away from us.

I'm writing to you as a black woman in society, but all you see is a Negro wasting your time. I'm extremely tired and so are millions of black people – exhausted of you affecting their lives with your hate like the pathogen you are.

Just to be clear, I don't hate you. I don't spend my days fearing you, like you do us. I shall not stoop to your level, but I will tell you that I give you all my pity. The 1950s are gone. Slavery is behind us and the 21st century is here, and we don't want you. We will not tolerate your vile actions of hatred any longer! Mark my words, we will stand strong and wipe you off the face of this earth so you can never hurt anyone again. I will not be a victim of your brutality. I will rise above your wicked ways of corruption.

Eight minutes and forty-six seconds.

That's how long you were on a black man's neck.

And I just have to ask. Why? Why… WHY? How could you do that to a human being, just because of the colour of their skin? Why do we have to march during a pandemic to remind everyone that our lives matter? What is so wrong with being BLACK?

We are not lesser, we are not insignificant, and we certainly will not be shot down because you infect people with your cruelty and stereotypes. Wearing a hoodie as a black boy should not mean a death sentence. Being a black man on a football pitch should not lead to death threats and monkey sounds from the crowd. Being black should not be so painful. We are not a different species altogether nor are we unevolved apes. WE ARE PEOPLE!

When people ask "No, where are you really from?" it screams ignorance which you inflicted on them. You crawled your way into the person's heart and clouded their judgment, making it rotten. We are human beings that deserve respect and dignity – something that seems to be lacking in society, thanks to you. I will never understand why you hate us – hate is such a sad thing to have, so I feel for you.

BLACK LIVES MATTER and you know it. You've always known that we matter, and that's why you hate us. You hate the fact that we are capable of being successful, strong, proud, and smart.

For too long you have been this dark cloud over our lives. We learned to live with you around, but now we are reaching past your cloud into the light, where freedom lives, and we are almost there. The higher you build your barriers the faster we will run to true freedom. We will not let you win this war, and I know you're scared. You will always be on the losing side and no matter what you throw at us, we will do our best to stay strong and not give you the satisfaction of defeat. A coward like you has no right to be here, so maybe you should "go back to wherever you came from".

We've been fighting you for hundreds of years – but this time you're the one looking over your shoulder.

Sincerely

Zoe Chinda

EMMA SPORTON, 17

Dear whoever you are,

It's like we are all in the same contrary old boat, isn't it? Since the coronavirus pandemic first became a thing, I haven't really known which way is supposed to be forwards, and even so, if what is supposed to be forwards is the way I really want to go. I feel so lost at sea.

I don't think anyone can claim the worst experience, though, do you? We're all probably withstanding some pretty tough emotions that, depending on who we are and what we've experienced, will each magnify themselves into something bewilderingly intense, confusing and irritating. Someone who is working at the NHS may be ready to break down into tears over the pressure of work in a world that is distinctly unfamiliar. Equally, a student might be constantly frustrated that communications with their tutors are no longer consistent, that there is such little clarity for what the next year will hold, that their future is still uncertain and there are not many people to talk to. Both are situations that effectively invite negative emotions, and I think it's important to recognise that there are so many situations across the country, let alone the world, that might be causing similar emotions, despite how large or small they might seem from an alternate perspective.

One thing about being cooped up at home all day is that you are much more aware of what's happening on the news; or at least I am. I think it must be because, despite our interactions with others being so limited, it's one of our only ways to connect with people. I didn't think I would miss something like that, but I really do. There's something really nice about being able to talk to someone: debating about some event that might be relevant to our lives, or might not be, and yet might resonate with us anyway. However, instead we are stuck in a situation where it is simply relevant to all of us, and we become simultaneously more aware of the news, and more overwhelmed by it. Looking after ourselves has become something that needs to be relearned, and it's been pretty clear that some people are stubborn about this. But people are stubborn about everything and anything.

I think what has become clear for me during lockdown is that procrastination is both beautiful and not at all useful. Communication is very difficult sometimes, but always, always worth it if you truly put yourself out there. There are so many wonderful people out there, both on and offline, family and strangers, who are doing everything they can to help in all sorts of ways. Whether it's making dance videos, songs, creative writing workshops, giving suggestions of new hobbies to take up, providing a distraction, making us feel a certain level of success; providing comfort. And people aren't letting any type of restriction stand in the way of what is most important to them. For example, the Black Lives Matter movement has taken up such a powerful stand over lockdown that it is really inspirational and inspiring to hear. I think that if someone needs a sense of purpose, it is encouraging to be able to see something hopeful as an incentive to keep going when it's tough.

I've rambled on about all sorts now. When I started this letter, I hadn't realised how much I actually had on my mind. It's nice to get it all out really, and hopefully let people know they aren't alone. I'm currently sitting at my laptop, trying not to overheat because the weather is pretty relentless at the moment. I miss being able to go to dance classes. I miss college. I miss my friends. I sometimes feel really cooped up, and yet sometimes find it overwhelming to go outside, I'm missing my old routines, which were jam-packed, but I've realised now how much I loved it. At the same time, I'm keeping my eye out for things to do, which is hard when sometimes I feel lost at sea, as I've said before. But something like writing this letter? Dear whoever you are, please don't let yourself shut everything out. The world is still turning after all. You'll find it worth not letting this world spin its web without you being part of it. Your priorities might have changed since this all began, you might have become more aware of your mental health, alternately you might be so busy that you've become less aware. But regardless, we should all remember to do what is best for us, and if that isn't schoolwork right now, don't let it stress you out. If that isn't the workout you told yourself to do, maybe decide if you genuinely want to do it or if it's adding more stress than you need right now.

I'm just a college student, so you don't have to listen to me, but we're all in the same contrary old boat that doesn't want to go the way we're trying to steer it. (Drink up this metaphor. I'm not letting it go, apparently.) It's probably best that we all try to learn from each other right now, so don't forget that this is all very difficult, and if you're struggling, there isn't a better excuse than that.

Have a nice day, stranger!

Emma x

"Within an anthology discussing solidarity, Emma Sporton's letter perfectly balances the line between capturing the emotions of the public, alongside the self. Exploring an emotive approach, there are moments of reflection for both the writer and reader, providing an opportunity to contemplate the societal effects of the Coronavirus pandemic. Emma imparts a subtle assurance of hopefulness for the future, with the ambiguous recipient of the letter ensuring that all readers can find this hope and sense of self within the writing."

Kishan Ganatra, Volunteer Editor

FREYJA HOLLINGTON, 15

To the written word,

Confined to the papered walls of houses that were only a place of transition. A place for the quiet parts of our busy days; we grow sick of our homes. Once there was a time when we would dream of these spaces; yearn for the mattresses of our beds. Pine for the cushions of our sofas. But all good things turn sour, sickening, when they are in excess. And when you can't leave your couch, can't escape your bedroom. You begin to seek the hum of busy streets, the productive thrumming of quiet cafés, the chatter of a classroom and the overpowering scent of coffee that perfumes the workplace. The mundane of everyday is no longer so tedious, when the everyday itself becomes abstract. Change brings fear, and so we want the comfort of familiarity.

But wanting these things does not do us well. In the end, life is different now, and no amount of dreaming can put us back in the office, the classroom, the café, or the busy streets. So how do we cope? Well, when dreary weather prevented us from enjoying our gardens. When the terrible Wi-Fi kept us from calling those we missed. When the channels on the TV no longer gave us what we wanted. You held our hands and took us to new places.

You had always been there: patient on the shelf or trapped

in a dusty box beneath the stairs, and we knew it. We had visited you before, captivated by your very nature. Enjoyed passing time with you beneath a chunky blanket, sipping a warm cup of tea. Yet we never fully appreciated you, not really, not until we were trapped ourselves. When the world was in chaos, we turned to your pages to find solace, comfort, and a place to escape crumbling reality. And you delivered. We saw new people, places, possibilities, and perspectives all through the lenses you created. We fought demons, solved murders, loved deeper than we knew ourselves capable. Cried, laughed, screamed, and shouted. Stayed up late to continue the journey, simply because we had not noticed the time passing.

You existed not just in the inky evidence of yellowing pages, but in the voices of those most passionate heroes. You were the blade for those who sought to fight injustice and inequality, never silenced by the confines of brick walls. You called out to us; allowed us to break the abnormal normality we had become frozen in. Inspired us. Encouraged us to speak up about the faults in society. So that when the cogs of the city began to turn once more, we knew what to fix. And what to break.

The papered walls of our houses were no longer so confining. The mattresses of our beds and cushions of our sofas not so frustratingly routine. We could endure the yearning for busy streets, quiet cafés, classrooms, and offices because they were no longer the places we truly wished to be. We found that, with you, time passed quicker. We enjoyed the days again and again. Each sunrise no longer like a tally on a cell wall, but the promise of something great and fantastical.

As we near the return to some form of normal, somewhere besides our homes, I hope we do not forget what you have given us. Though we may restore you to the shelf, to the box beneath the stairs, we will always understand the greatness you hold. Appreciate your brilliance.

Thank you.

"To me, Freyja's letter represents the transformative power that books will forever have on humanity. That whilst the present may look bleak, they will always be there to soar us above our four suffocating walls into mesmerising worlds, as they have since time immemorial."

Callum Roome, Volunteer Editor

JAMES COWTAN, 17

26th October 2020

Dear Mum,

I know we didn't see eye to eye during lockdown.

And I know I tend to bleed on people who haven't cut me. Sometimes I worry that they might leave me because they're all bloody, so I wanted to write my experience and struggles of coping with the coronavirus pandemic to you in a letter.

Before lockdown began, if you would have told me that I would have needed to complete all my college work on a computer at home and I wouldn't actually have to go into college… well, I would've jumped at the chance to just work on my laptop at home!

But I can tell you now that I took everything for granted.

Because of the pandemic, I was robbed of my time at college – and as a young teenage lad who was recovering from depression, doing nothing all day, every day, wasn't good for me. I would sit in my room, watching the clock tick by every painful hour. It was like my mind had been sent to an execution.

There was a moment in lockdown where I was sitting in my room, feeling so down. I thought that everyone's goal in life is happiness, and yet the end result is always death? So, what's the point in walking barefoot down this road of shattered glass when you could just skip straight to the end… What seventeen-year-old should be thinking that?

There were days when I would just sit looking out of my window at the rain and hear it tap, tap, tap on the windowpane and drip, drip, drip down onto the conservatory roof. And there were days when I just sat on my Xbox, bored out my mind but still laughing and talking with my friends, masking my emotion. The issue was I couldn't really complain, because everyone was going through the same problem: stuck indoors all day because of a virus. And I thought how stupid it was, but what could I do? I was helpless – it was like I was stripped of my freedom and my recovery, and just left to rot. I was a sinking ship that was burning at the same time.

I saw on the news that a nineteen-year-old girl committed suicide due to her fear of losing her independence. She went down as another suicide statistic of mental health and she, unfortunately, was not the only one. There were other people, like me, that felt tranquilised with waves of stress and fear crashing over them. Before lockdown, I had the ambition the size of an elephant and I had things arranged like birthday plans. We even had a holiday to look forward to in Spain, but we were just stuck in the house instead.

I had the same routine every day.

Get up. Brush my teeth. Go downstairs and whinge to you. Go back upstairs. Watch that same old clock tick past every hour (and quite frankly the hours felt like they turned into days, but I still stared at that clock). Eat dinner.

And I took it all out on you and Dad.

I used to shout, because I was so frustrated that I couldn't do anything but sit. Having me in a bad mood added to all your other stress, such as a new-born baby and two seven-year-olds who were so very afraid of what was going on (they weren't old enough to understand the seriousness of the issue that was happening worldwide). This continued for months until Boris Johnson announced that we could at least go on runs, and I did, whether it was just a mile… or two… or three… I just wanted to get out of the house. I then felt as though I had part of my life back.

It made me realise that an unhealthy life like that was not the sort of life I wanted to live.

Yes, we are still in this pandemic, and the second wave is now upon us, but I don't feel suffocated to the very brink of me falling unconscious. As the year has progressed, I've seen my friends. I've been to college. And it's all so refreshing, compared to what lockdown was like when I felt as though I was breathing in the same air I was exhaling. Plus, I'm not now trapped in a room like a prisoner in solitary confinement.

It feels good to have a part of my life back. At least, for now.

From James

P.S. You're back home now, surrounded by the people who love you the most and you're over 50 days sober, which you should be very proud of.

ALEX CANE, 18

Dear World,

Hello, it's me, Covid-19. And this is my message to the world.

As you may know, I am the reason why many thousands of people are becoming terribly ill. And in some cases, people have died. You must be thinking why on earth did I decide to start a global pandemic? Well, let me tell you…

First of all, I would like to tell you some things that may change your opinion about me, as everybody either calls me horrific names or is just absolutely terrified of me. I don't blame you, as I can easily kill you… if you're unlucky. Did you know that since the early 1930s the world population has increased from 2.3 billion to an astonishing 7.8 billion? From 66% of wilderness intact to now only 35% of wilderness. We can see that the world is changing: humans are dominating other species, taking away their habitats and ecosystems. You are destroying this for your own benefit, but what you are unaware of is the damaging impact that emanates from what you do. The more you take from the wild, the faster you kill it off. So, that is where I come into play.

Seeing as you humans keep breeding uncontrollably like pests and destroying the world you are living in, I thought I could stop you and kill some of you off. How many of you have lost a family member to Covid-19? That must have been extremely painful for you. So why is it that you can just sit there and be oblivious to the world dying off from pollution, destruction and climate change? All these things are happening, and nothing is being done about it. So, unfortunately, I no longer care who dies or not. You can't even follow the rules to prevent me from attacking you, never mind opening up your eyes and realising that, without nature, the human race would become extinct. Maybe not in your lifetime, but sometime in the future it could happen.

As I float around from place to place like a jellyfish in the ocean, I see many people suffering from my negative effects… but have any of you actually been wearing masks, staying two metres apart and washing your hands? The amount of people I see walking around that are not social distancing or being cautious is unbelievable! You cannot blame me if you become infected. My job was to wipe out half of the human race in the hope that it would restore some life into nature, to prevent the extinction of animals and humans, and to stop animal species being hunted and killed for money and food… for what, exactly?

As you may know, coronavirus started because people in China were buying bats from the food market, regrettably passing on this dangerous virus. Infecting many as if it was a replay of the Black Death, which spread across the broad and tempestuous seas without any knowledge or awareness of what was to come. I hope this teaches you a lesson to stop being the murderous monsters that you are, killing animals just to make some money. It isn't just bats getting killed; other species – many of which are on the brink of extinction – are murdered every day just to be sold for each of the different parts of the animal. This more than likely has some madness story behind it, like the tales of the Kraken or the Loch Ness Monster, believed by many. For example, shark fins are cut off and put into soup: this has been happening since the 10th century, as they were originally eaten by emperors as a means of exhibiting power and wealth. But as we know in modern days, there is no scientific proof of this. Yet people still continue to cut off their fins to earn a huge amount of money, risking their lives to not get caught in this evil act, but also risking the sharks becoming extinct, leaving them to die slowly in the ocean. Why, I ask, must you continue to do this just for your own benefit, when you know the myths aren't true?

However, I would like to apologise to those who I have affected mentally. I can imagine how lonely you must be, not being able to have as much social interaction with others. Or maybe you are struggling financially as businesses shut down, and you lose out on money which you need to support you. And sadly now it isn't there anymore. Many of you just sit indoors all day, moping around feeling depressed or isolated. That isn't what I wanted for some of you! However, I do have a few suggestions which may cheer you up. For starters, why don't you go out and explore nature, reconnect your soul and body to the earth and get yourself some fresh air? Second of all, you should grow some plants: this will keep you occupied each day. Having something to remember to do every morning will give you a good start to the day, making you feel happy knowing things are making progress and that you are caring for nature.

Thirdly, why not do some yoga? This will prevent your body from becoming stiff, like the movement of a robot when it hasn't been oiled. Since you're not being as active, it's important to focus on your physical health by doing such things. If you don't keep active then your body is not releasing endorphins (these are chemicals that make your body feel good) which improve your self-esteem and reduces the risk of anxiety and depression, which a lot of you must be feeling during lockdown.

So really, I am not as bad as I seem… Open your eyes and really take in everything around you. Don't just sit there and complain that you can't go out or do the things you are now missing out on, when YOU are the ones who are responsible for the ongoing global pandemic! Change the way you live, and maybe you won't have to keep facing all of these misfortunes that are happening.

Yours sincerely,

Covid-19

ELSPETH WHITE, 15

Dear whoever wants to read,

Is it just me, or does lockdown have a smell? For me it's the smell of a very specific soap or the smell of paninis cooking on the Foreman grill (a welcome change from school lunches). I know it's cheesy, but it's really true: when I use that soap or eat that panini, I swear I am transported back just for a minute.

The thing is – and I feel guilty every time I confess this – I feel nostalgic for lockdown. I know it was terrible in some ways, and I know we're not really out of it yet, but, if I'm honest, lockdown kind of showed me how I want to live!

Wow that sounds depressing: being isolated and unable to even go to restaurants, but there are so many things I wouldn't change. Online school, for example, has taught me self-study suits me! Apparently I thrive off silence (or the gentle hum of traffic from the dual carriageway) and independence. Also, as sad as this sounds, I think I thrive off only seeing a select few people (on Zoom calls, etc) a couple of times a week. I am definitely exposing my introversion here.

Perhaps time has slightly warped my positivity about isolation here. In the first couple of weeks in September, seeing friends and teachers was invigorating and genuinely helpful. It's still great now; it's just sometimes I crave my desk: my escape.

I speak from a privileged position, in that no one I love has had the virus, but, in retrospect, I liked – dare I say loved – lockdown! My motivation was, for the most part, high (thanks to Joe Wicks) and my lockdown routine solidified pretty quickly. Five school lessons a day, insert breaks with piano in the morning, Disney movies at lunch with the odd Zoom call, and you have a genuinely happy Elspeth!

You know, all the days in lockdown have sort of blurred into one, but a day I can remember very specifically is the first Sunday of lockdown. We'd just been on a walk (which is a remarkable jumpstart for my imagination) and once we were home I found my empty, beautiful notebook and began to write. There's something magical about writing for me. It removes you from time and space for a couple of hours and builds an entire universe out of strings of letters. A pretentious way of saying it, but there you go.

The point is, lockdown fuelled a passion I never would have discovered otherwise, and for that, I am forever grateful. Another passion that lockdown introduced to me was the wonderful world of cinema. I reckon, as a family, we watched films five out of seven days a week. We watched some classics like The Truman Show, some underrated gems like About a Boy, and some questionable films too (cough, cough, Dodgeball). I loved every minute of it.

I think the truth is, the positive things stick with me rather than the negatives (which is great!), but at the same time, it kinda makes lockdown feel fictional. I don't think 2020 is going to sink in for a while to be honest.

Thank you for reading my random stream of thoughts,

Elspeth

BECK SEWART, 16

Dear Mr Brown or, as I know you, 'TLMaths',

You don't know me at all. I am not one of your students, or a dedicated watcher of your channel, or even a lone unread commenter on one of your many videos. I may be responsible for the addition of several days to the total watch time on your channel. However, I doubt that in these unprecedented times that this would be the biggest thing on your mind.

But I feel like I know you very well. I have watched the way your classroom has changed, as posters came up and down and your whiteboard circled from dirty to clean and vice versa. I feel that I have enjoyed the full range of your Math Pun T-shirts, and I have been the victim of your unpausing but short lectures, hundreds of times. Looking at the numbers, it would appear that I have.

Me and my closest friend found ourselves in the same situation as many back in March. Facing five months free from any responsibilities, but unable to do anything with that freedom. So we found solace by sitting down every morning in front of a webcam, pen and paper in hand, ready to conquer a year's worth of knowledge with nothing but reckless abandonment.

Surprisingly, we succeeded.

Your A-level Maths playlist is 1005 videos long. 499 of those cover the AS syllabus, making for 46 hours 51 minutes and 3 seconds of content to work through. Don't worry, I didn't count them: coding is the other love in my life. Of those 499 videos, we watched a surprising number. My notes could probably fill a textbook, though my actual revision of the concepts… Well, some things I should leave for next year.

But we watched them.

We spent more time with you this lockdown than any of our teachers, our other friends, or even any other YouTuber. We ooohed every time we saw a video with your new intro. Groaned every time you covered something we were sure we knew, and then fell out of our seats when you showed us a new way to do it. I still remember (only a few months ago, can you believe?) when you reinvented proving a prime number, and we had to pause the video in amazement.

Everything suddenly seemed so simple.

This lockdown was not simple. My sleep schedule broke, and I have no idea how I'm going to be able to keep up with the slog of A-levels after 5 months of nothing of the sort. But you were the one constant in all this.

10:30, every weekday.

Thank you.

(a fan)

RICHARD BROMHALL

CITY OF LITERATURE

Dear Sainsbury's Meal Deal,

I loved you, no question. You know that, don't you? It wasn't only the satisfaction you brought. You were there for me, and you know it too, don't you? As I ascended Hockley and Goose Gate each lunchtime, I knew you were waiting, ready to continue our love affair: tearing of bread, crunch of crisp, hiss of unscrewed bottle top. I would sit back in my chair and, for a few brief moments, life was perfect.

But then March arrived. I worked from home, and when the restrictions came – 'you can leave the house for one hour's exercise every day' – I had no choice but to comply. Where was my nearest Saino's? Over half an hour's walk away! And I couldn't get to you. I wanted to, desperately, but I wouldn't have made it back in time. We used to see each other every day, so this long-distance relationship was tough. I promised you I would be loyal, and I meant it, but then something happened: I met Shakshuka.

She's from Morocco. She's healthy. And she can even be cooked as a vegan option. Because of her, I've lost weight, I've got more energy, and my work rate is up – no more sluggish afternoons now, my love! Does she satisfy me in the way you do? You know she doesn't. How could she? But she's better for me. We both know it, and she contains something special that you, quite frankly, do not: sophistication. She's got cumin seeds, smoked paprika, and SAFFRON. She melts on my tongue, and delightful baked egg adds a deep taste of which you could only dream. Could you ever give me that, Meal Deal? You know you can't. I'm moving on. I have to. And as much as you tempt me, I must resist. We were good together for a time, but it's time to put it to rest, my sweet.

Others will devour you, and as much as I will always love you deep down, there's nothing I can do, so forget me Sainsbury's Meal Deal, and move on.

Forever yours,

Richard (Nottingham City of Literature)

ABBY STAFFORD, 17

Dear my dedication,

Some six months ago, when blooming Spring rose past the cold soil and set my hand in motion, I sat happily with friends beside me. The air between us was warm like the Summer we'd never have, kept close to our skin as we leant against classroom walls, shoulders pressed together.

Sharing, I think, warm cappuccinos to ward off what little wintery spell had choked its way through the brightening sky. Whispers of a far-off storm kept clear through our silly remarks and happy laughs.

We wrote, not knowing, all of our experience, our work and our hope into little blinking documents that would never find themselves completed. There were a lot of things to do: work and study and applications for anything and everything that could take us to our futures. Little did we know.

Because when time paused like that blooming Spring had forgotten its way to Summer, our futures too forgot that every day was still a day in our lives that fell forwards into the wind. And the breeze that took them stayed unforgiving of our crumbling teenage years.

But it was fun. It was exciting. Weeks could fly and we were happy to see them leave, to feel the break in pressure as every responsibility charmed itself into vanishing.

We'd been so busy preparing for so many different, so many 'necessary' things, that to hear our empty schedules from our empty rooms was a breath we could take with us.

Somewhere in that timeless void, where the seasons disobeyed the days I'd watched burn out like flames, it became so easy to just – stop. Because as I sat, alone, in a cool kitchen with a churning laptop flesh against the counter, I could see clearly my friends sat across from me, video outlines pressed together whilst I stayed apart.

Blinking documents shut their eyes and I closed my writing fist. Lessons too far away to attend left absent as June fell into July. Work and study and applications for some delayed future could wait, I decided, because if it wouldn't come then there was no reason for me to go.

Hobbies, too: such fickle things. I left them with the Spring. With nothing to do or see or say to help the time return, it kept on its way.

Yet somehow as the seasons return, as Autumn rears its head, I sit again in a classroom with friends whose two metres I cannot tread. Timelessly, the world has changed, and expected me to as well. Deadlines come and I still don't go, because I think I've lost the reason. If everything can stop at will, why would I stay in motion?

Sincerely,

A student.

CHARLOTTE LANES, 16

To be read in October 2070

Dear Future Self,

Is it easier now? You will be reading this as a 66-year-old woman. So, tell me – I'm dying to know – do you still have the crippling, dark, emptiness feeling of being trapped, like you did in 2020? As if you can't breathe from the comfort of your own home, from being stuck in the same place for months, just so our families could live another day.

I do hope things are better now…

So, is this everlasting war from Covid-19 finally over? If so, who won? Do you now get to have the exquisite taste of freedom once again? Can you finally go into the shops without the choking, thick, warm air from the mask you were forced to wear everywhere you went? Can you finally walk the streets whenever you want to, instead of feeling like a caged animal, like you weren't allowed out of your cage unless the owner (in our case the Government) would decide to let us out? How is Mum? Did she lose her job like her boss said might happen? Same with people all over our country – did a lot of them lose their jobs too?

How about food? Can you remember when people were panic buying and so there wasn't really any food or toilet roll in the shops? Did this happen again? Do you remember that day when your mum had to tell your siblings they might not be able to eat fresh foods or proper cooked meals for a while as there was simply no food you could find in the shops? How about the pure anger and fear it gave you from the selfishness of other individuals not thinking of other families, and the humour that millions of people took part in on social media putting a spotlight on the situation of… toilet rolls. What about the 'Eat Out to Help Out' scheme Boris Johnson (our Prime Minister) made to get 50% off your food, where the Government paid for the other half, if you ate out? Even though, in the current time of me writing my letter to my future self, this is one of the main factors why we may be going into a second lockdown right now.

Has your mental health improved? Do you not feel like there are chains binding you to your house, and every link from those chains are the people who have died from this treacherous, deadly disease? Even though, at this moment in time, the Government are making people go into lockdown, no one is used to feeling like a trapped mouse being tested on, with no escape. How is that going to have a positive effect on people's mindsets? Do you remember when we wanted to be out having fun with friends and do normal things an average 16-year-old would do, not being stuck at home, hoping and wishing to escape the prison that was your bedroom – but couldn't? Unfortunately, only when it's safe enough to do so: well, is it still like that now?

Also, if you are reading this, by some sort of miracle do you actually now have a boyfriend or husband? Do you have children with someone, or even grandchildren? Have you told them the stories of the events I went through as a 16-year-old, like your grandparents used to tell you? Even though, right now, I've still got 2 months until I'm 17, what was it actually like on your 17th birthday?

But it wasn't all bad! Exams were cancelled: this was fantastic because it saved me from the stress of revising, when all there would have been to do otherwise was wage a war with my textbooks and my pen and paper! Every cloud…

I hope, future me, whenever you're reading this, you finally have a better life. I hope you're not still incarcerated at home trying to save people's lives and preventing the spread. I also hope that this coronavirus hasn't affected you too much and one day you finally get back to normal. And that we have all been set free from this living hell!

Yours sincerely,

Charlotte Lanes

DANIEL MACDONALD SMITH, 25

People are dying, friends and family, alike; and the vilest virus we are pitted against isn't biology, but the baseness that forces us to fight one another while forgoing our humanity.

LUCY PHILLIPS

Nottingham Trent University

Hello,

Funnily enough much of my lockdown has been about writing letters to people I don't know, and now here is another one!

Getting post, real post through the letter box, has been a highlight in these socially distanced times. Since the start of lockdown, I have received all sorts of treats. An anonymous friend sent a chocolate bar in an unsigned note; another posted a packet of sage seeds, which are now planted and sprouting; another sourced the most amazing 3D pop-up card; and my sister-in-law sends prizes every time I win the family bingo on a Sunday night (three times, since you ask). Knowing that friends and family are thinking about me has provided real solace.

And whilst I too have been writing the occasional postcard or sending random gifts to friends, I have also been writing to people I have never met before. I opted to take part in the Nottingham Playhouse Pen Pals project. This means writing a letter to someone you don't know and may never know. Writing such a letter presents a series of quandaries. Why would a stranger want to hear from me? How do I write a letter that is interesting and engaging when I only have a name and two words of description? Does it seem a bit big-headed to just ramble on about myself? But then what else is there to say? I can ask a question or two, but there's no guarantee I'm going to get an answer. Does that matter? Maybe I was overthinking it! I decided to keep my letters short and to stuff them with as much goodwill and good humour as possible. In the end, it felt good to reach out and I really hope that the two women I wrote to feel a connection and recognise that their letters were written especially for them.

I have also been writing to a friend's daughter. I don't know her, I just know we are similar ages (in our early 50s) and she is in lockdown in a city 50 miles from here, with only her carers for company. She is unable to see her partner or visit her day centre, and is understandably frustrated with social isolation. Jigsaws are proving to be a great distraction, but as she has limited dexterity she prefers ones with no more than 100 pieces, and the pieces must be a good size to handle, not too small and fiddly. Local people, through Facebook and our neighbourhood WhatsApp group, have donated jigsaws and every week I send her one or two through the post with a note. Last week a friend who lives on the south coast sent three brand-new jigsaws for me to post on to her. Her dad tells me how delighted she is and I'm ultra-excited to be able to connect with her and hopefully I will get to meet her one day.

So, my letter of solidarity is about connection. Connecting with friends and with strangers, and the benefit that brings us all. It's simple. It's often the small things that matter.

I hope that whoever reads this has stayed safe and well, and has been able to stay in touch with loved ones throughout.

Best wishes and take care

Lucy

LEANNE MODEN
CITY OF LITERATURE

Dear January Me,

I hope you're doing ok? How are things back there in the past? Your hair looks nice.

I know you feel excited about all the new projects you have lined up for 2020. It's going to be a big year, but not for the reasons that you think. You're always chasing the next thing, and the next thing and the next thing, and that's great. But don't forget about the stuff you already have.

Visit your parents as often as you can; go swimming every day – even when you don't feel like it. Take your cousins to the park as often as possible. A lot is going to change this year.

Remember that good things come in many different shapes and sizes and that, every time one door closes, another one opens. I'm not saying this to be pessimistic, I'm just asking you to keep an open mind. Sometimes the biggest disappointments are actually opportunities in disguise.

Don't be afraid to experiment. Mix things up. Try something new. You're always going on about doing something different with your hair, and you never do it! Be brave. There may be days when you want to scream at yourself and everyone around you. Don't. There are some things in the world that you can't control. Focus on the stuff you can change.

Make friends with your neighbours. Help out the couple that live upstairs. Thank the postman. Make sure everyone around you is ok. Your kindness is your greatest strength. It always has been.

Remember that standing out, being different and speaking up for what you believe in is tough, but necessary. No one ever did anything amazing by staying in their comfort zone.

Hug your friends as tightly as you can. Focus on the good things in your life: you've got your health, and a roof over your head. Plus, your hair looks nice.

You have the power to change your behaviour and become the best version of yourself, and that's the first step to changing the world. It won't be easy, but be brave, and wear your heart on your sleeve. You can do it. And you've already come so far. I'm so proud of you.

Take care. And if anything goes wrong this year – if you make any mistakes, come up against opposition, or your plans don't go the way you imagine – remember that nothing lasts forever. Hair grows back. This, too, shall pass.

Lots of love

Future Leanne

(The one with the bright pink, side-shaved hair!)

EMILY, 16

Dear me,

If you are reading this, then today's date is the 22nd of March 2020 and you are preparing for your upcoming GCSE exams. Tomorrow the prime minister will announce a national lockdown to fight the recent Covid-19 pandemic and reduce the spread of the virus, so I thought I would offer you some advice for the next couple of months, because, like it or not, life as you know it is going to change.

Whilst we are on the topic of change – which, ironically, was the brief for your drama exam – one thing you will notice right off the bat is the amount of spare time you are about to receive. A whole six months of it. I know it sounds like a dream come true, but it can turn into a nightmare if you're not careful. The second thing you will notice is that you will procrastinate, a lot. Also, you know that hair that took you so long to grow out, and that you said you would never cut off? One missed hair appointment ended up with you cutting your hair twice and then colouring it fourteen times, so have fun with that. Was it worth it? I'll let you figure that one out on your own.

Even though this lockdown period is good for you, growth-wise, you miss out on one of the most important things in your life: your friends. Suddenly, you go from seeing your friends every day of your life, going to dance for hours and constantly being surrounded by people who you adore with your whole heart, to lying on your bed, in your room, alone. The plans you made for the next three months of your life are completely derailed. Your GCSE exams get cancelled. Your motivation drops and you find yourself in the place you most feared you'd end up. After a while, the distance from your friends becomes too much and you find yourself replying later and making people you'd talk to for hours on end into complete strangers, and that's okay. One thing you learn to accept is that life isn't always perfect, and it isn't always sunshine and rainbows and that's okay.

Remember, this isn't 'the end of the world' that people will make it out to be, but if everything starts getting too much and you start to feel overwhelmed, think about this time in your life as a transition, a new beginning. You won't know what it is – as I'm writing this now, I'm not sure I do either – but we will get through this together no matter what happens.

Sincerely, me.

P.S. Don't message your ex, because you will get hurt, and make sure you let go of people who are holding you back. Your heart will thank you later. x

LAURA STANLEY, 22

Dear all the therapists,

In lockdown, I have not learnt a new skill
but I have watched too many films and shows
starring Lesley Manville. Days before
it all changed I saw her bewitch the stage.

You asked me what makes me go on living.
I miss live theatre. I miss running
to London when I feel like I'm burning
down to my last candle wick and I miss

sitting in the theatre's breathless dark
and I miss how the words place me under
a glass jar and I miss the rush of fresh

air after the final scene and I miss
stepping outside into the foyer light,
relighting into a flame from a spark.

– Laura Stanley

The writer Maya Angelou famously said: 'If you're not angry, you're either a stone, or too sick to be angry.' She encouraged people to 'use that anger, yes. You write it. You paint it. You do everything about it. You talk it. Never stop talking it.' Our next letter is in the spirit of Maya Angelou's words and contains information that some might find distressing.

CHINENYE OKOLO, 16

Dear Generation Z,

I am so proud of you! Look at how much we have accomplished this year. We have caused an uproar all around the world and had people screaming: "BLACK LIVES MATTER!" We all did our part, whether it was by going to the protests, donating money, signing petitions or spreading awareness. Everything that has changed in terms of the mistreatment of black people is because of us and our efforts. However, so many more black deaths still haven't achieved justice: Breonna Taylor, Taylor Rice, Eric Garner and many more. Did you know that Taylor Rice was only twelve years old when he was killed? Did a young boy deserve to die for playing with a toy gun? NO. He had many more years ahead of him, and instead, his life was taken away by the people that are meant to protect us. The Black Lives Matter Movement has not been forgotten; it wasn't merely a trend. People are still angry, and we have every right to be.

All these killings happened because of racism. All the people mentioned above were black. However, nobody talks about the troubles of the Asian community. Everyone has normalised subtle racism towards the Asian community; they gave up fighting. That is not okay! It's not okay to refer to Asians as 'bombers' or to pull your eyes in a funny angle to humiliate them. It's not okay to steal their culture for profit by appropriating their cultural clothing. That is not okay; we need to stop normalising racism towards Asians. The worst thing about it is that they suffered so much abuse and tolerated harsh words because of the coronavirus. That is not fair. Yes, you can be angry that you must stay indoors, or cancel your plans, but look over these past few months and tell me that you haven't developed and changed for the better. Without this quarantine, black people would still be silently suffering.

So many injustices occur all around the world, not just in the USA! Shukri Abdi, a Somalian refugee, came to the UK in the hope of a better life, away from the conflict in Somalia. Instead, she was drowned at the age of twelve. The reason I cry about this case is because her death wasn't the act of adults – it was the act of children. These children manipulated Shukri and told her they would teach her to swim, but instead they left her to drown. Children did this, all because Shukri was Muslim, which made her 'different'. The judges ruled the death of this innocent child as an accident, but Shukri was subjected to bullying several months before her death, which her school was aware of but did nothing to end it. Young people should be enjoying their lives, not bullying others or 'jokingly' threatening to kill someone if they don't step into the river to 'swim'.

The fact that I even have to write a letter about this is disgusting. If you cannot see anything wrong with anything

I have written here, you need help. If you are not enraged by what you have read, you need help. If you are not motivated to enact change, you need help. If you are aware of such incidents and yet do nothing, you need help. I am a sixteen-year-old girl who is preoccupied with adult problems. I shouldn't be doing that; I should be worried about my GCSEs, not worrying about whether I will live tomorrow because I'm black, or whether my friend will be killed because she's Muslim.

Black people have suffered. Muslims have suffered. Asian people have suffered. We do not want to suffer anymore. So, Gen Z, if you're reading this, what are you going to do about it? Let's go out and make some noise!

Yours Faithfully,

Chinenye Okolo

P.S. Be kind to others. You have no idea what they are going through. Be better than the people around you, and let's show those so-called 'adults' that we are not too young to understand these issues.

"I chose Chinenye's letter because of her raw and unfiltered discussion of racism and xenophobia. She explores racism towards the Asian community, which is often overlooked and normalised within our society, and challenges people who are complicit."

Daria Paterek, Volunteer Editor

MEGAN TURNER, 23

November 2020

Dearest mind,

I have spent the longest with you throughout lockdown, despite numerous attempts to escape. Returning to you in my room after every pause, back on the sofa when FaceTime finally ended. Less usual distractions, more time alone.

Thinking of all and everything or staring gormlessly at whatever was going on just past the front gate. Stopping to look at nature and learning to be less busy, nothing to delay. Only living in the present because, at the moment, the future feels cancelled.

Remember when time felt still? When the only reason you were sure it hadn't stopped was the ticking coming from on top of the fireplace. On those long days in the depths of April, practising taking deep breaths felt like the only way to get through it. But you did.

Now the year is nearly out. Some say time flies when you're having fun, but no one tells you how fast it ticks on when seemingly stationary. Make sure you get out of bed; it will help your head. And don't worry if you write loads of lists that never get looked at again.

It has never been easier to disappear in public. Summer

2020 said: "sunglasses and masks". A different life between where you could have been. Light years away from the new year in Amsterdam. A million miles away from memories made before March.

Going through the front door, just to get out. Out to the post box and up to the park, pounding streets to feel the breeze against your face. Has your anxiety calmed?

Remember the hours spent walking around parks and the week you left food out for the squirrels? This could never be lost time: think of the words you have written, the books you have read, every place they have taken you and every word you have said. We had no choice but to make friends with each other.

I wonder when everyone will be able to get together again. Only the future can tell. But not getting close enough to touch, with curfews and bubbles, brought loneliness into focus. It is scary living through a pandemic, not to mention knowing you will be part of the generation paying back for its aftermath.

It isn't time that makes situations feel better, it is an understanding. Social media created circles and expanded safe spaces. Posting about weird moments and memes raised a smile. Truths shared, a summer spent learning about world histories and societies systems. Most importantly, a desire to change and switch things up for the better.

As the future passes, I hope you get a grasp on the post-pandemic climate.

Thank you for being by my side, my closest confidant. Until the end of this, or the start of the that… and every moment in the middle… I will see you on the other side.

Megan, almost out of her mind.

"This letter really resonated with me as soon as I read it. During lockdown, I struggled, like many people, with my mental health. Trying to stay afloat amidst a global pandemic was difficult when I felt like I was drowning in feelings of loneliness, my university assignments and not being able to see the people I love. Our relationship with our mind is the most important one, one worth working on and one that will stay with us no matter what the world throws at us next."

Emma Stirland, Volunteer Editor

LIAM SKILLEN, 22

Dear Reader,

I don't know how to start this letter. I was not prepared for a worldwide pandemic, and I am no more prepared to write this letter. Many talk about lockdown or the virus as if it's in the past tense, but for many others – myself included – it is still very much the present. I don't think I will ever live my life completely in the sun again. It will always be overshadowed by coronavirus. It will always be shaded by a dark cloud, mockingly hanging over my wrinkled 2020 diary.

"A worldwide pandemic, how exciting!" I thought, as we closed down the cinema I work at, and we all took goodie bags of food home (and ridiculously large bags of pick and mix). All the wonderful things I'd do! I had never had this much free time since the school summer holidays. I always wasted them watching TV reruns and playing on my Nintendo DS. Maybe I'd terrorise a frog in the garden pond for an afternoon before returning to my adolescent cave. But, unlike that simpler time, I planned to actually do something this time around. The pottery and print-making class I signed up for may have been cancelled, but I could create at home. I could bake all the sweet treats I wanted (pre-flour shortages of course).

In truth, it was never likely I would achieve *everything*

on my to-do list. I have a habit of asking too much of myself. I'm not sure if it's the goal-orientated Leo in me or my Catholic upbringing, but if I'm not being productive then I have failed. Output must be the priority. Friends and family always ask, "What have you been up to?" and if I have nothing to say I overflow with guilt. Almost as bad is only being able to repeat the same old routines. So, each week I would do something different. Learn to ice a cake (properly), macramé a plant hanger, weave a mini tapestry, complete an online course. The list goes on. And whilst initially these were all things I wanted to do, I didn't enjoy them. I was no longer doing these things for my own enjoyment, but simply for the gratification that comes with productivity. Even outside of work I orbited a false calling, the need for yield and production.

I found some comfort in my new role helping a couple of households with shopping and errands and such. I had a use. Well, on Wednesdays at least…

I walked around the supermarket with purpose, foraging for those hard-to-get items. My friends and I shared locations with certain supplies still available.

"The corner shop on Chesterfield Road still has self-raising flour."

"The Polish aisle in Tesco has something that translates to cake flour."

You could generate status just from your knowledge of certain groceries.

Again, I found myself in the role of provider, attempting to care for my friends who lived close by. We couldn't see each other, obviously. I would bake for them almost every week, a small gesture but it was the most I could do. If cake and cookies don't bring a crumb of happiness, then I don't know what does. And to those unfortunate souls who chose to abandon my small town for universities in the big city, I attempted to send regular postcards and letters; small envelopes filled with stickers and other relatively flat objects. No one would be left behind. This was my new life purpose.

Rising tensions at home made for a less than ideal situation to nurture my delicate mind. Normally I avoided this by going to work an hour early to sit in the staff room, getting the train to Nottingham and drinking a chai latte in the Waterstones café, or simply wandering the supermarket, pretending to take interest in a jar of 'the best' olives.

But I was stuck. Nowhere was open. The pressure was killing me. I would drive around aimlessly. Once, I attempted primal scream therapy. I'm sure the friend that recommended it was joking, but I needed something for relief. Anything.

I'd never felt so lonely. I'd never felt so hopeless.

As we are now returning to society, I am even more terrified. I wonder if this is just another nail in the coffin for a jobless generation. Educated but unemployable. Well, maybe not *unemployable*, just unemployed. Not by choice, of course. The only thing I want right now is a salaried job with a half-decent pension. But despite all my worries – throughout it all, as usual – my friends have been my pillars of joy and hope.

For now, all I can do is hope for a better future. I hope I can read this in the future, full of freedom and joy.

And I hope you can too.

All the best,

Liam

ANASTASIA M, 14

Dear world,

I am writing as Coronavirus, hoping that we shall all understand why 'I' am here on Earth with you.

Firstly, I came because I have had enough! Enough of you torturing your nature, your environment, your creatures. Enough of your carelessness towards other lives. More animals are endangered, more than there have been in centuries. However, humans just ignored this. Ignored that the grass was more littered than ever! Ignored that they did not have the fresh smell of mowed grass! Ignored that fewer birds and animals were heard and seen. Humans ignored that the world was getting too polluted. So, for their own good, I came.

Secondly, I came because I had enough of you fighting and arguing about nothing, splitting up for the most immature reasons. Entertaining yourselves with the internet, instead of your mountains. Instead of your beautiful views. I came because arguing had indeed got you far, but the wrong far. The bad far. Far, as in hatred and greed. Humans have reached a peak I thought would never occur, so I came to sort it out.

Then I came also for your families. You have forgotten about them. You thought seeing your family was sometimes even embarrassing. You took it for granted. Going to a restaurant, transfixed with your phone. Hogging your electric devices, instead of a welcome conversation with friends and family. You have forgotten what it is like to enjoy your family, very few humans still know. So I came to make you feel remorse and make you feel sorry. Sorry for your merciless mistakes. I came to show you what it is like to be apart from your family. I put you in lockdown so that you could understand how much you love and treasure your family; how much you are loved.

I came so that I could put a stop to your polluting. As you were in lockdown, nature freely spread its friendly wings across Earth once more. More birds came to sing goodnight and good morning at your windows. The fresh smell of nature woke you up. You were not there to pollute Earth anymore.

I came, but I will have to go. I have also caused alarm and many deaths, and that I am sorry for. But there is no other way to teach a human. I came and I will go, leaving behind hope and peace. If I don't, I will be forced to come again.

I leave behind me the hope that will keep you united.

From your 'would-be enemy'

Coronavirus, also known as Covid-19

"This letter portrays the pros and cons that Covid-19 allowed us to face. For instance, we never thought about the value of having a family and people caring. It is also amazing how a letter of 400 words can show us what we were not able to see one year ago."

Rijuta Lutchegadoo, Volunteer Editor

MARTA SILVA, 18

Dear World,

We are all facing really tough moments right now. Since the beginning of the year, we have been exposed to a lot of changes that have not only affected our lives, but also the way we see the world.

Ever since we've been stuck at home during lockdown, challenges have always come to us. Every month a new obstacle appears, making everything more difficult to handle. In a situation where all of us need to help each other and stand united, I thought humanity could finally improve.

Unfortunately, such a thought was only a dream. A moment when everybody could unite and help each other turned into a moment when everybody only attacked each other and became more distant. If humanity can't learn from the deaths and sickness around the world, what more is needed for us to become better?

Where is the empathy? Respect? The love for each other? Can't we learn those basic things now? When did we become so selfish? When did we only care for ourselves and not for others? When did we become so empty?

Yet I still believe we can becomc better. This year was one of the hardest in our lives, if not the most. But the year is not over yet. We can still change.

My message for the world is to hope for better times. But this cannot happen if we do not start making things right. All of us are going through hard times and we need to keep together to become stronger.

Marta

MILLIE BONFIELD, 16

Dear Future Self,

Well, what a year 2020 was!

From celebrating the New Year in London, watching the vivid fireworks with no worries, to three months later, when a war had begun with Covid-19. Can you remember the last time you could see your friends and grandparents for months? 21st March. Two days later we were all in prison.

Can you remember playing monotonous board games with your family while waiting in the kitchen for the next announcement from Boris Johnson telling us how many lives coronavirus had taken that week? That was when it started to hit that Covid-19 really had dented the world. Can you remember having BBQs constantly because there was nothing else to do on the balmy summer days? Can you remember dying your hair and buying endless amounts of clothes just because of boredom? These months were the strangest ones of everyone's lives.

Remember the last day of school and our last waves of goodbye. It was all just one big rush. We had a day's notice that our goodbyes to everyone – for what seemed like forever – were only a few hours away. Taking parting photos and actually being able to touch our friends for one last time for months. Remember being sat in the assembly room full of wet eyes from watching the end-of-school video. Remember being told prom was going to be cancelled (one of the most special nights known for a sixteen-year-old) after weeks of excitement and planning with your friends.

But the worst of all was not being able to sit your own GCSEs after years and years of preparing for them. Do you recall Boris announcing GCSE and A-level results were going to be from teacher predictions? Although it was good in some ways, with no more stress of revision, the stress of waiting took its place. Waiting for months and months to get that email of our results and not being able to distract yourself. Knowing that your future was no longer in your hands, but in your teachers'.

It was good in some ways, having time to yourself and having time to reflect and getting closer to the three people you were with day in, day out. Although your sister was annoying and you did bicker with your mum, your dad always tried to calm it all down by replacing the bickering with activities to occupy us.

Anyway, its 2040 and you're thirty-six now. Wow! Do you have kids? Are you married? I hope everything is back to normal and Covid-19 is long gone. Do you still have to wear a face mask in public places? Remember sweating underneath your mask? Well at least it hid your double chin. Is hand sanitiser still everywhere in sight? Although the majority didn't even bother to notice it was there. I hope you achieved your dream job and I hope you're having the best years of your life. We got through the worst!

Best wishes,

Your past self,

Millie x

NINA MOELLER, 25

Dear pupils and recent school graduates,

I wanted to start this letter by writing about the immense pressure that comes with being in your final year and finishing school. But much more important is starting with this: it is going to be okay! You are going to be fine! I know, that's easy to say. And yes, even though it is easy to say, it doesn't mean that things are tough until they work out fine.

But trust me, you will be fine. Just hang in there.

This was a very troubled summer to finish school. Did you get asked a lot about what you want to do after school? Or did you not get to do what you wanted because of the exam results fiasco? Or because your travel plans were destroyed? My sister is in her final year now as well, and when we speak about school I remember all the pressure that mounted on us from every side. Did you study enough? This is going to be hard, so brace yourself! What are you going to do after school? Where have you applied? I very vividly remember being in the same situation. Everybody made it sound like it was the most important decision in life, the thing that would define the course of your working years up until your retirement.

And this, from my own experience, is simply wrong.

Whatever happens now will not define you. You can change

your direction anytime. Don't listen to all the voices that tell you otherwise and make you doubt yourself. Your parents are worried about your future, but what they advise you says more about their outlook on life than about yours, or your abilities and grit to make things happen. Having a perfect CV matters less than you think. If you can convey enthusiasm and are willing to invest work, that counts more than many 'fancy'-sounding internships on a sheet of paper. Don't lose yourself trying to optimise yourself for a specific profession. If you stick with following things that you enjoy doing or see a purpose in, you will take one step after the other naturally.

You will look back in a few years and there will be a trajectory, a thread that links it all up. Maybe you sit here now and think "I'm okay at things, but there's nothing I really excel at." The truth is that most of us don't have that one thing that we are better in than everyone else – and that is fine. People that are good at several things are much more needed: so they can manage, bring together and mediate between different areas. Maybe you currently have no idea what you want to do and don't see how there could possibly be a thread one day.

Think about the things you truly care about. Not necessarily fields, but skills and mindsets – do you like bringing people together? Or dig yourself into something and don't let go until you get to the bottom of it?

Are you good at planning? Are you observant and notice tiny details, or does it make you happy to do something that has an impact on others? What I want to say is that you have skills you possibly don't even think of, merely because they are not subjects that are taught at school. Trust me, there are many things you are good at which you don't see. Many things are also simply up to chance and luck. Maybe you start talking to somebody on a train station, who then wants to partner with you or hire you. Maybe you move to a new city and suddenly become involved in new hobbies that will influence you. You never know, and that's okay. Go with the flow.

And this will help get you to where you want to be. Maybe you find a subject or field that you discover you love. Or change course along the way and find out that there's something else that you are better suited for, in which case the thread is your pursuit of what fulfils you. It's all okay: nobody really knows what they're doing, and we can all only make an educated guess. The paths that aren't perfectly straight and smooth are usually the more interesting ones, and you may well carve out a life for yourself that is a bit unconventional but fulfils you. In any case, don't worry too much about it now and don't stress!

I was extremely anxious when I was in my final year, seven years ago, because I desperately wanted to get it right, but nobody came and handed me a recipe for success. But guess what? It all worked out so far. My thread is that I love art and history, and this has guided me since I finished school because I just couldn't let it go and it wouldn't let me go. I've had good and bad days, successes and failures. There are fascinating people I have met, and wonderful places I've been to, that made me find out more about myself and what matters to me in life. I fulfilled the dream I've had since I was young, of moving to the UK. Here, now, I can look around and see many little things that make me very happy and proud of myself and where I've come to. Looking back, I could have saved myself the anxiety and just had a little more faith that it would work out. This will be the same for you!

It's a bit of an overworked concept, but if you do something that makes you happy and that adds value to your own and other people's lives, you'll do it well, and that will guide you.

Best wishes,

Nina

PATRYCJA SKRZYPKOWSKA, 25

Dear Jane,

You are not going to believe how desperately devastating the coronavirus is for me. I am struggling to make a scant living during these terrible times, and anybody who says otherwise is just a fool! Honestly, I feel like I am drowning in a deep, dark sea of loneliness. I know that you are absolutely outraged at the suffocating situation in the country right now – just like me.

But I need to share my huge hurdles with you.

You know how incredibly hard it is to study and work concurrently. Imagine that you can't find any part time job… it is absolutely impossible to stay afloat! Only yesterday, I was reading a recent survey which stated that 60% of people are overqualified for their jobs due to the coronavirus. Meaning fewer workplaces for other people that are less qualified or educated. I am finding it very hard to travel to Poland at the moment, and I miss my family achingly. I know it is possible to buy a plane ticket now, but they cost an enormous £200 (when normally they are a fraction of it)! So there is another lonely Christmas for me. How wonderful!

I did manage to get a decent job with good pay during the early stages of lockdown. I gained invaluable experience working in the hospital, and I finally felt able to sail free – financially – in what had previously been a sea full of despair. I felt that I was doing something vital for society, and it gave me enormous energy to keep pushing on. Unfortunately, I then had to go to college. As a consequence, I was not able to swim in the sea of prosperity anymore.

Now I feel that I have a tremendous amount of work to do when it comes to my current education. I deeply regret that time spent working, when I could have filled the gaps in my education. Now I must work extremely hard to achieve and obtain the qualifications required. I don't really feel prepared to study at university. Yet I am applying for it…

Furthermore, I think that the Government could do much more to help those in need and provide support, even after lockdown. For instance, they could throw the vulnerable a much-needed lifeline. Now the coronavirus cases are increasing like overwhelming waves, day after day. Maybe something will change, because locking down all the companies is not a sensible solution.

I hope that you were not left to the sharks in your industry.

All the best,

Patrycja Skrzypkowska

TEO EVE, 23

Dear Lockdown,

You've not been so bad – though you've been one long moment suspended and dangled over the city. A spring and summer gone, traded in for the worst seasons. Every hint of opening brims with optimism that seems undeserved. Just four/five/six months ago we watched China through hazy screens, were shocked by Italy while still being relieved that this wasn't happening to us. Lockdown, you cause envy of all the other countries for whom time has resumed, while we still watch shops through queues that spill into the high street.

The thing I miss the most is being able to wander around the streets, winding my way through them without a purpose. My world's not my room anymore – it's not been that bad for months, but I only leave the house to shop. All else seems irresponsible.

I thought I'd have tons of time to catch up on all the things I'd missed, culture that can be consumed at home, reading in the garden. Work has swallowed my time, made it disappear. It feels as though I'll emerge from this with nothing to show for it, as though I've not survived. That's what I've got to show for it. That's what we've all got for sitting inside: the chance to come out of this alive.

We must remember those who were forced to work, and all the lives lost of those who caught the virus before we were told to stay indoors. We must commend those who, during a pandemic, took to the streets to protest the injustices and inequalities seen in today's society. Without urgent action, these inequalities will only grow as Britain leaves you, lockdown. We must all continue the work we started during this worst-of-time.

Lockdown, you were terrible. I have missed my friends and my family. Lockdown, you were not a prison. When doctors and nurses tell their stories, I hope that Parliament will listen.

Teo Eve

TY HEALY

Dear Optimism,

Initially, I thought to write this letter in Braille, because for as long as I can remember you have always been blind. However, this has never seemed to be a disability because I've never known another so wide-eyed. I miss that… I miss you.

You used to live at the forefront of my thoughts: always redecorating my mind with bright colours, approaching new challenges with no fear, taking pieces from these lived experiences and placing them like furniture, to create the perfect feng shui. I'm still a person seeking balance but I think I need your help again.

I wrote a little poem for you:

This current form of me is a shell of a former me
Pessimistic wondering through the mystic fog
Trying to hear the sound of a tree falling in the woods
All the while knowing that no one is around to cut it down
Was that my optimism refusing to social distance?
It's close, it's about two metres
Just not close enough for me to feel it.

I know this is not my best work, but I hope you get the point. I need that blind optimism back because, with age, concern also grows. Grey hairs sprout from the mind's grey walls, remember? You haven't been around to paint with the bright colours. Sorry, I have this tendency to use metaphors to dance around the topic at hand. In reality, I'm not sure what to make of it.

We had to plan my aunt's funeral with the current laws in place, no more than six people present at the burial they said. We had at least 20 people there who felt like immediate family and, believe me, we could have washed our hands with the tears.

Optimism, maybe you haven't been around because your energy was transferred to my aunt. The strength that Claire Moran-Healy displayed through her fight was both inspiring and enlightening. Never scared, she was only sad if she saw that we were: that's the kind of person she was. Our family let yellow balloons float to the sky in her memory, I can only hope that the optimism she had for us to stay strong and keep supporting each other will eventually fall out of the sky and land back into my mind. That thought alone warms my heart, and that's a start.

I am optimistic enough to believe you will read this letter, so deep down I think you're already with me... You always have been, as she is. As I look in the garden and see the yellow balloon tied to the gate, I smile. See you around.

Forever Grateful,

Ty Healy

RACHAEL HAMILTON-PEARL, 16

No matter where you were or who you are, being quarantined affected everyone. Companies big and small were losing money. This caused people to panic as this was their life, their futures and it all was falling apart. Although all of this was going on, the one thing that helped me get through was knowing I was helping everyone, including the people I love stay safe. No matter how hard – it was for the best.

CJ, 17

Life in Lockdown: What Was It Like?

Life in lockdown was extremely stressful for me. I was constantly worrying about the near future: what will happen to others, and how will we recover from this. I have had medical appointments cancelled due to this deadly virus. Appointments that could have helped me and change my life. As a 17-year-old I shouldn't be worrying about the internal problems I have. With the support I receive I should be feeling relaxed, right? Instead I'm always on edge about what's going to happen next. Will I get my issues fixed? Do I have to wait another year? The stress was just constantly building up, weighing me down. Crying for most nights not knowing what to do. The lockdown felt like a lifetime not being able to see friends and family members. Being isolated from the world made me feel depressed, outcast, forgotten. However, the lockdown did help bring my family and me a lot closer. We managed to bond, relate to each other and express ourselves. Despite the inner isolated feeling I had, I felt so happy being surrounded by my loving family. I felt gleeful, loved, and cared for. They supported me when I was feeling like I was low all the time.

The hardest part of lockdown was the breakup with my boyfriend of eight months. Not being able to see my friends, I felt so broken. I wasn't able to do my regular activities. I couldn't eat, sleep or even drink. I didn't want to leave my bed. I stopped playing video games, I isolated myself even more. It was hard to talk to people. I didn't want to touch my phone, my laptop, nothing. I didn't want to have contact with absolutely anyone. I wanted to be alone…

But it didn't take me long to spark back to my usual self. After the messages and support I received, I started to smile again. Regardless of how hard life can get, there will always be people behind you to support you. I came back to my social media, messaging people and even making new friends to play video games with. It helped me out so much! I started to regulate my diet, maintain my weight and just become a better person than I was before. For once I actually felt happy being who I am. Now I get people saying how I inspire them to become a better person, starting with getting rid of toxic people that have been weighing them down.

Even though I was feeling happier, there were more obstacles coming my way. Constant flush of emotions, anxiety, depression. All these emotions and expressions I hid away from others. I kept them to myself. It was extremely painful not wanting to tell people because I was scared I'd bother them. I always put a brave face on like nothing was happening. I slowly started to express myself by opening up to my family and friends. No matter who you are we all have our struggles and issues. Smiling through the pain doesn't work and you should definitely express yourself. Don't worry about bothering people – they're there for you for a reason! I made so many new and amazing friends during this lockdown. It's definitely a memorable memory. An odd memory I must say. 2020 may be a terrible year but I think we all have something to take from it. Care for those around you, look after yourself and be grateful for what you have because you'll never know when it will be the last time you'll see it.

CHRIS STIRLAND, 17

On March 23rd, Boris Johnson announced something I never thought I'd experience: England was officially locked down. Meeting friends, going to school, and not wearing a face mask all became illegal overnight. At first, I thought nothing of it. I thought in a week's time England would be back to normal. I couldn't have predicted how wrong I would be.

I went into lockdown with an optimistic mind-set. However, that optimism started to fade as each day became longer and longer. Life became very meaningless, as the weeks went by with no real end in sight. Although staying connected via social media really helped me out, and keeping up to date with what my friends were doing with their time during lockdown inspired me. They were dealing with it a lot better than me: they were having productive days and were enjoying their time in isolation. Whilst I lacked any motivation to get out of bed in the morning.

Gradually, I became more and more aware that if I was ever going to enjoy lockdown, I was going to need an end goal to work towards. And although to many it would seem pointless, I set a goal to get better at a video game. Having an end goal really helped me get through the struggles of isolation. Being in isolation also made me begin to appreciate the small things in life, such as simply being able to leave the house and visit my grandparents. Loneliness was a recurring theme when discussing lockdown with my friends; no one was prepared to be stuck inside for five months, and that was very evident just a few days in.

Whilst I managed to get through the lockdown, there were many that were lost due to mental health issues and suicide. Personally, I don't think there was enough done by the Government to help those out who dealt with things like depression during lockdown.

STACEY SMITH, 17

To all of our loved ones,

First of all, I want to say how much I have missed you all. Being apart for so long, it proves how much you mean to me. The fact that I could only see you through a screen, it hurt. The only way we could talk was through the phone. There was no meet up, no family days out planned. Within seconds it was all taken away from us. It feels as though we haven't done anything in 2020. No memories were made which we would hold onto for the rest of our lives. Nothing special happened, no celebrations, nothing. There's a pain in my heart to think of what we've all been through. But the truth is, we have done something this year. We survived. We survived it all.

Lockdown hands-down has been the worst experience of my life. Being isolated away from everyone. Constantly looking at the same four walls of my bedroom day in and day out. Life felt as though it was slowly slipping through my hands. I couldn't catch a piece of it. Lockdown was keeping me captured in its cage, isolated from the world. I couldn't do anything. The beast that is Covid-19 had taken over all our lives. We became its prisoners and there was nothing we could do to escape. The anxiety and the fear swirled around my body. It was always looming over me with no escape in sight. The days seemed to draw out longer as we followed the same routines. The boredom followed onward, dragging out longer every single day. It hurt – it hurt so much. The pain was too much. Life had been swept away from us and there was nothing we could do about it.

As lockdown continued on, we saw people try to carry on. Banana bread and chocolate brownies seemed to fill our social media screens. Late-night Zoom calls kept us connected, with family quizzes and meals prepared for us all. We tried to keep the positives high to mask out the heartbreak in the world. We stayed at home for those around us, as NHS workers powered through the months. They helped to save our loved ones – the true heroes without a cape. But we can't forget the other key workers who helped keep our world afloat and running. Carers, policemen, firemen, supermarket workers: they all played their part during the pandemic. We will always be grateful for those people. They fought for us on the frontline. They never stopped working even at the hardest moments and to this day we show our love and support towards them.

But one thing I will always be grateful for, is the support I had from my mum. We had a great bond beforehand, but now we're even closer. She is my best friend. She hugged me when I was down. She sat with me as I cried all the pain out. She kept me smiling at the worst moments. But one thing she always did was love me and my little brother and keep us safe. To us, she is our hero. She kept us on the path ahead. We all had someone who kept us going, and for me my mum was my rock and world. I couldn't have done it without her by my side. And I know how lucky I am to have her with me.

2020 is slowly coming to an end. A year that will forever go down in history. The year the world fought Covid-19 until the very last breath. The fight continues to rage on, but all we can do is hope and pray. With the positive thoughts, we all still hold on to, we hope that this nightmare will soon end. As we slowly move on with these last few months, we will soon be in 2021, all we can ask for is to stay together and hope we can move on with our lives and be happy once again. My thoughts will always be with those who have lost someone to Covid-19. This year has truly been a hard one. Having to fight with the beast alone but also struggling with mental health has to be one of the hardest things. Battling a disease which is slowly taking over the world and now fighting your own battle. It starts slowly suffocating us, becoming more and more painful.

I'm thankful for those around me and I'm thankful for those who have never stopped during this pandemic. We all joined together as one in order to save our lives. We will forever be grateful for those times where we smiled during these hard times. Every Thursday night when we clapped to show our appreciation for the NHS. 2020 will go down in history for what we faced this year. Covid-19, countries in lockdown, plus the other events that occurred this year. We have lost so much of our lives, but we can only look ahead at the bright future that is heading our way. We will find a way out of this. We will find happiness again. And we will reunite with our family and friends soon.

Thank you for everything and the support throughout 2020.

Stacey Smith x

YERENNY CA, 25

NYC & Nottingham
September 09, 2020

Dear Lukas,

You have been my security blanket ever since I moved to England from New York City in 2018. You showed me how to take transportation around Nottingham and explained why everyone seems to make a line for everything (which is so unlike Americans). I became complacent; stopped showing you just how much I appreciated you. After all, I was making new friends at school now, and while we had our movie nights whenever time would allow, I was the one that usually ended up having to apologize. "Sorry, last minute shift at the care home," or "Sorry, but I ended up signing up for X event which will have X important person, and you know that I need to network for my career! Rain check?" These became normal words to leave my lips when dealing with you.

I am a New Yorker; we learn early on that if we aren't busy then we are being lazy, and that's just not acceptable. Our worth is only as high as our to-do list. When I wasn't in lectures, I was running to do 14-hour shifts in order to pay for my tuition and rent. Food was a luxury; water becoming my best friend. I can still recall when lockdown came to England. At the time, I had started feeling unwell and didn't have the strength to go out and stack up on food (or toilet paper, remember that shortage?). My depression decided that it wanted to come back to haunt me. Motivation was suddenly gone; I would spend hours staring blankly at my walls with too many thoughts in my head… and then you started FaceTiming me.

In your usual Lukas manner, you greeted me with sarcasm (which is what makes us such great friends), but then you saw I wasn't feeling too well; that I appeared to be exhausted. From that day on you made sure to FaceTime me every single day. (I've checked, you really have been calling me every day since then!) It was the little bit of interaction that my dark mind needed after so much free time in this new world. All of my school events had been canceled; I couldn't go to work due to my compromised immune system, because of my severe asthma; and all of my international friends had run back to their country at the first hint of this scary virus.

Thanks to you I got the energy to fix my room; to start taking showers again (depression takes every prisoner that it can, including hygiene, sadly) and brush my teeth. I would wake up early and go downstairs to make my daily smoothies and mashed potatoes with gravy. Then I would journal, meditate for at least an hour and listen to my favorite motivational speakers on YouTube. By 5pm, as always, you would FaceTime me with a smile on your face and tell me a story about something that happened in your day, during your daily one-hour run or in your flat. It gave me the strength to help my flatmates turn our living room into a gym during the day, and at night switch it into a movie room, where the three of us laughed as we watched movies and commented on them.

You gave me the strength to work on my YouTube business, where I read tarot cards and expressed my thoughts. To deal with the stress of online learning; we had to learn independently. As technology issues enjoyed arriving and interrupting that small window of contact.

In June, I had a business plan to write but just didn't have the motivation to do it. What was the point when I didn't even know what school would look like next year, let alone if I would be able to afford to come back as an international student? When you found out, you dragged me out of my house (by now we could visit each other's homes) and sat me down on your couch while you worked and had me write my business plan. You walked me through the pages upon pages of numbers for my financial sheets, and then drove me to Heathrow airport since I needed to go back to America. A mixture of circumstances, from my brother having contracted Covid-19, as well as the fact that I could no longer pay rent as I didn't have a job thanks to this pandemic. I couldn't tell you then, looking at you from the passenger side, that I am so grateful to have such an amazing friend like you in my life. Who would have thought that an aloof person like me, who rarely talks or likes to go out, would have stumbled upon someone as kind as you?

I can still remember the look you gave me the last time we saw each other face to face. We were unsure if I would ever come back to Nottingham, as every country was in lock down mode. You waved at me; I waved back with my face mask already on. You were told that you couldn't go inside with me; only passengers are allowed inside airports.

I walked through the abandoned-looking airport. In the past, it would have been packed with people trying to reach different destinations, but now it was empty with the few staff and passengers that were there. Half of their faces covered with a face mask and gloved hands. I had on my face mask that I designed myself which said *'I can't breathe'*, in honor of George Floyd who was a victim of police brutality. You hadn't been able to understand why everyone was risking their health to protest in the Black Lives Matter movement. I had shouted at you for not understanding, but how could you? Your skin was pale, your eyes were bright. You've never experienced what it's like to walk into a store with eyes on you, to be kicked out of a place due to the color of your skin – but I have. My dark curly hair and dark skin made sure that I always stuck out.

Sorry, you know how I get distracted. As I was saying, I walked through that abandoned airport, using my mobile to check in (a measure taken to try to reduce contact with others). Security took seconds and as I walked around, wondering if there would be any stores to buy some food, I saw that they were all closed. Inside the airplane, everyone had a mask on, and food was brought to you in a box among row upon row of empty seats: proof that the pandemic was here. To think that in late June a plane to NYC would fly so empty. I spent 8 hours with a face mask on, and when we finally walked out of the plane our temperature was checked. We had to give a form saying where we were staying, and where we were told to quarantine for two weeks.

Once more, I began to lose contact with you; a five-hour time difference would do that I supposed. You still called whenever you could, checking up on me and asking how things were in America. After living in England for two years, coming back to my country was a bit of a shock. People walked outside with their face mask on but seemed to ignore the six-foot rule. Buses had canceled their fare, which led to bodies being pressed against each other as we traveled from point A to point B. Everyone seemed to forget how this virus spreads.

Time Square was no longer packed with tourists; now it was practically empty. Only homeless people could be seen now, and a few locals walking around. There were notices on stores saying that they were closed due to the pandemic, restaurants apologizing for not being able to offer seats inside. Was this how we would live from now on? Afraid of physical contact? It felt as if the world was now seeing what was inside my germophobic mind. Now I was no longer seen as odd for wanting to use gloves to open doors, or constantly use hand sanitizers. I was no longer seen as weird for not wanting to hug someone or kiss them. The world had been forced to catch up to my way of living, to become a hermit like me. Who would spend my days locked up in my room because I couldn't be bothered to socialize.

A month after moving to NY, I got some news: the place that I had lived in for a year was raising rent, and a 12-month contract was asked of me as well. Due to these times, unemployment was normal, and I couldn't find a job to afford the new rent asked of me, so I needed to move out quickly. I reached out to you, panicking, explaining what happened and saying how I would have to move in with one of my friends, but I didn't think I'd have the time for that.

You casually offered your office space to me; rent at your place would be much more affordable, and I'd only have to share it with you. When you did that, I wanted so badly to break down and cry, to tell you how grateful I was to have an amazing friend like you and how much I love you. But instead, I simply said, "Thank you," and wondered if you really wouldn't mind living with me for the next 8 months.

A few weeks later, things became more tense. You ended up having to move out my things to your place all by yourself, while working your 9-to-5 job from home. All without complaining to me, telling me that it was alright. While I stressed and panicked, you handled the whole situation calmly; thanks to you I didn't become homeless. I have a place to go back to when school starts, and I even look forward to it.

This pandemic, it brought us back together. It taught me who were my real friends, and who were the people that just wanted to use me. This letter is to let you know how grateful I am to call you my friend. It's not much, and I don't think that a lifetime of telling you how grateful I am will be enough, but it's a start.

From the bottom of my heart, thank you for being my best friend.

JYC

LEWIS, 16

After finishing secondary school not being able to sit my GCSEs, the whole country was put on lockdown following the rising number of daily cases. At first, I thought this was exciting and adventurous: it felt just like a thriller movie. No school for months, lazing around the house all day doing nothing but playing video games, it was everything I ever wanted to grow up. However, as the weeks of waking up midday with no passion or targets to achieve, it started to irritate me. The same four walls around me every day. My bedroom was no longer a place to escape society: it was a prison cell I had found myself spending all my time in. I had already rinsed Netflix of all its content and got bored with everything I used to enjoy doing in my spare time. I couldn't go to live events such as gigs and football matches, which were both a big part of what I enjoyed doing in my spare time, I was restricted to seeing family members on opposite sides of windows and only went out to go to the shops to get the week's food supply, this is when I decided I needed to start being active and setting myself targets.

I began by doing 5k runs mainly to maintain my fitness and take use of the hour fitness rule set by the Government. This gave me an opportunity to escape from the continuous time loop I was living in. Furthermore, I decided to start biking places such as down the canal and onto the River

Trent to expand the temporary world I lived in. I found myself communicating more with my friends and family and, when the time was right, spending time with them, as I started to appreciate everything around me. I slowly began to realise the society before was gone and the only way forward was adapting.

Lewis

AMY BRADBURY, 19

There's just over a month left of the mental countdown which I've had since the 12th of March and I'm very ready for it to be over so I can get back to some semblance of what living actually feels like. Until then I will have to continue with the philosophy that has served me well in everything from the last twenty minutes before home time to having all my plans cancelled by a pandemic. This is that: the passage of time is the only certainty in life. With time comes change and this change is usually for the better.

RYAN LOUGHLIN, 16

This was supposed to be the summer where us 16-year-olds could relax due to us finishing our GCSEs. Instead, we were met with more rules to follow and no fun in sight. What we saw was a world that we didn't fully understand yet we were plunged into chaos. We were at the pivot point between understanding the gravity of the situation, but not being able to do anything – because in the world's eyes we were still "kids". This year has been very difficult for the youth of our country; we have to worry about our families and our grandparents and anyone else in our family and, just like a prison, the only way we can talk to them is by phone.

You would have to be a blundering buffoon not to realise that the coronavirus pandemic has affected the education of children and teens alike in the most severe ways. It has affected all ages differently: students in secondary school have been lost in the jungles of responsibility and have had to take it upon themselves to learn an entire year of school curriculum – basically unassisted – because teachers were not able to see them do their work because of it all being online. This also meant that many students didn't see the point and couldn't see the future positives, so decided to either do the bare minimum work required... or they just gave up. This is not acceptable! Students need to be pushed by teachers to reach their full potential. It must also be very difficult for young children who may only just be going to school at a pivotal part of their social learning when they would usually make friends, but instead are sitting behind a computer screen not being able to make those incredibly invaluable connections. I see this as a big problem in the future, as we will have children that may come out of lockdown not knowing how to socialise: that will have dire consequences on their later life.

ELLA MUSGROVE, 17

Despite lockdown and going months without seeing friends, I wasn't lonely or isolated, as I used the months to work on myself. I re-read books – like actual paper books. I spent more time in the garden, even if I was only listening to music, and I went on a walk with my sister on a sunny day down a local nature reserve trail. Because of the lockdown, I really connected with my family, even if sometimes it ended in a screaming match. I still kept in touch with some friends, and it really became clear who I'm friends with. By keeping in touch, I mean by spam-sending funny gifs and YouTube videos about rubber ducks and the FaceTimes that were so soul boosting.

I didn't realise how much I would miss my typical college day, running for the bus and walking through the town centre, and feeling euphoria when one of my teachers let us go early and I finished my college day as it started, once again running for the bus. And before I knew it the lockdown was over, and I was getting ready to start my new course. But the change in us shocked me after months of people helping each other. People went back to attacking each other – whether that be online or in person. We became better people once and we can do it again, and it should be permanent. We all have the ability to help each other and be kinder, even if it is a random act of kindness, for example giving a homeless person a sausage roll and a tea or helping a family member to order something online. The lockdown made us stronger, even if the people hit the hardest don't feel it yet.

Just remember we're all stronger now and you aren't alone.

Ella

RED SMITH, 20

To the family of my house, I miss you. Mum, Dad, Beck and Kitty. Mum, I'll see you when you take me home with Dad, hopefully we can go for a Caribbean. I don't really need to say much to you except that it's all love, it always has been and always will be.

LATOYAH, 17

Dear insecurities,

You once had me wrapped around your toxic rope… belittling, doubting my self-worth, making me believe I'm worthless.

Until I broke free.

From being constantly at war with my inner self, I finally let go. Enough was enough. There were two paths I could take… let you control me, shape my mindset, give me a negative view of myself and the world or take back my body and love the skin I'm in… count my blessings. You're no longer blocking me from great opportunities that come my way. You're no longer in control…

LUCY HILL, 18

Dear My Dance School,

Lockdown was hard and although you have me through many hard times before, this time you couldn't. For many of us, dance is a way to express our emotions, yet this was the one time we couldn't do that; the time when we were going through the most.

RHIANN, 17

I am such a strong believer in everything happens for a reason and I'm certain you will be exactly the same. From the bad moments now to the bad moments in the future, just remember it's happening for a reason. And of course, the good moments!

HEKMAT HASAN, 18

From the moment you are born, time begins dying. If you don't use it properly, you could lead yourself to failure in life. We have 365 days in a year. If you do just one hour every day working on what you love, whether it's studying, business or sport, then for a year you've done 365 hours a year. Those hours are the gap to success. Many people these days feel very lazy and unmotivated. There are many reasons for this, but the main reason is that they are unorganised. This comes when you don't have a plan. To make everything easier, plan your days. Set your goals and put a deadline. Each day you wake up, you will feel a lot better and motivated to start your day and finish it successfully. Think again and decide how you would like to live in the future...! Do you really want to be successful, or do you wish to keep your dreams unachievable?

FAITH, 22

These past few months cannot be changed, but they can be accepted. It has been hard, but it has been real, and you've never felt more determined to feel alive. Take what you've learnt from this time and use it to make the best of the time you're given. But don't forget to look around at how beautiful it is to even exist. We will see each other again.

SOPHIE GREEN, 16

22nd October 2020

Dear Prime Minister,

Isn't the coronavirus a horrible thing? Well, it's been difficult for us all. Not being able to see our families, not seeing our friends, and being cooped up in the house not being allowed to go anywhere. All apart from one type of precious exercise per day. But it has been most tough on the young people of the country, not just yourself and your age group…

The younger generation has it toughest at the present time. Lost learning time, not sitting our A-levels or GCSES: how can life be that prejudiced? How can young people possibly come back from this? Well, of course we will try, if you give us a chance, instead of casting us aside like a piece of rubbish on a landfill site.

Due to the coronavirus, companies are reducing the amount of people they hire. The amount of Covid-19 cases are still growing, like the rising tide of the ocean. This means people coming out of university who want to find a job are having terrible trouble because of the desperate economic situation. How do you think they feel about not being able to find a job? Do you want the young population to find a job? If so, think about what they are going through and don't assume they are being lazy. They already feel like a plastic bag floating in the ocean; they don't need the adults to remind them of their failures, which leads me aptly to the next point.

The coronavirus has taken a toll on young individuals' mental health. This is due to them not being able to go anywhere, see their friends or see their family. How do you think you would feel in their shoes? Do you think you would be able to stay positive throughout the whole pandemic? No, I don't think you would be able to, would you? So, take it easy on young people. Take it easy on them, since they need saving from the drowning tide of the ocean.

On the other hand, those who oppose my point of view would say that the Government have helped the young generation in this country and that money for mental health or jobs has been made available in spades. Moreover, there were other demands on public funds because businesses and the elderly also needed support. Unfortunately, there isn't enough to go round! Well, I believe that without looking after the young people, there will be no future for the country and it will go to rack and ruin without us. Because our talent will be wasted, and we will be rolling around like empty bottles at the bottom of the ocean.

To summarise, young people will be able to come back stronger with governmental support, we can do better than ever before once having emerged from the coronavirus pandemic. Youths will transform from a piece of plastic swirling around in the ocean into a majestic swan. Please consider supporting us, we need your help, now!

Yours sincerely,

Sophie Green

ELLIE GREEN, 16

Dear Covid-19,

I hope you are happy. All the lives you devastated. All the celebrations you ruined. I hope you are happy.

You sent the world into a mass panic when you started stealing lives. Lives that were not yours to take. Toilet paper and pasta went flying off the shelves. The UK was sentenced to lockdown just because of you, you silent killer. Over a million deaths were caused by you. Why do you have to be so cruel? Everyone wants you to leave and stop hurting us. Why can't you listen? You have already taken enough.

Students in the UK missed out on everything. We missed out on sitting our exams, partying at prom with all our friends and leavers' parties. The results which were given to us were unfair and some students were even robbed of opportunities just because an adult did not give them the right grade. It is all because of you. You caused all these problems for us. You made us students miss out on the most important time of our teenage years. We will never forgive you.

The hardest thing you caused, that I had to deal with, was not seeing my grandparents. I used to see them every day of the week for different things. But you made it impossible for me to see them. For me to abide by your rules of not passing your illness on, I could only see them through the window or over FaceTime. That is something I should never have to do.

You ruined everything and stole anything you could including the lives of one million innocent people.

The world will never forgive you.

Ellie

We started with Emani and now we end with Amina's letter. The idea of finishing school ties in nicely with the end of our collection.

AMINA, 16

Dear Me,

Your college teacher, Matt, set this as homework. As far as homework goes, this one isn't the worst. You are currently in your first year at college, doing a multimedia journalism course. You're liking it so far. Your teachers are good, your classmates are nice, and you're not overworking yourself to the point of extreme fatigue.

Your brother is getting married. You're happy for him, even though he annoys the hell out of you sometimes. You like his fiancée; she's nice and it's easy to talk to her. It's still weird that anyone would want to marry your mess of a brother. Oh, and, you're also in the middle of a global pandemic.

You were upstairs finishing your notes on a physics practical when your phone blew up with messages. You skimmed them all. Exams are cancelled. You think it's probably a hoax or something. You check everyone's Snapchat stories. They're all the same. The Education Secretary officially announces that GCSEs and A-levels are cancelled.

Everyone walks into school the next day, confused as the head teacher guides everyone into the assembly. Your last day is tomorrow, you don't have to work anymore, and you have to end an iconic period of your life. Questions are asked regarding the trips we all paid for, shirt signings and our final assembly. The day flies by. You and your close friend sit on a bench beneath a tree at break. You used to sit there every day for lunch, until a bird pooped on your friends. The last day passes, filled with banter, positive vibes and loads of photos. Everyone is given the letters their Year 9 selves wrote about the future. Of course, yours isn't accurate at all.

Then you go home, scrolling through everyone's Instagram posts and stories. You don't cry; you just sit in your stinky school uniform, reminiscing about the past and the future. The laughs, the late homework, the cuts and bruises in technology, and the new and scary changes you're about to face. Only a few days later, the country went into lockdown.

You loved the majority of lockdown. Especially Ramadan. It was simple and quiet. You'd wake up late in the afternoon, pray all your Salah (prayer), cook new food and stay up until Suhoor, watching random shows on Netflix. When Ramadan was over, you also did loads to keep occupied. You re-read Harry Potter, deep cleaned your room, watched various nostalgic films with your brother, and improved your clothing choices. Seriously, never let Ami (mum) buy your clothes again.

But then there was the other side of lockdown. The constant checking of the news to see how many lives had been taken that day. The Black Lives Matter protests after the death of George Floyd, which brought to light the discrimination against black people all over the world. The last-minute announcement that Muslims couldn't celebrate Eid, even though Johnson is considering letting the British public celebrate Christmas.

So, I think you'll agree with me when I say 2020 is the worst. I also think you'll agree with me that 2021 won't magically become better. I believe change will come, but we're going to have to wait a while for that to happen. Anyway, how am I doing in the future?

From,

Amina